Contents

What's on the Internet?

The Internet is a gigantic information resource, which is visited by thousands of students every day to help them with their homework. It is packed with data, pictures, news and all sorts of useful stuff. Nearly all of it is free to access, and it's available right now to aid you in your research. If you use it effectively, your homework will become more informative, fact-packed, interesting and eye catching. All you need is access to a computer with a telephone connection.

Are you new to the Net?

If you are new to the Internet you may find it confusing at first. For a start, you may come up against a lot of jargon and unusual terms, such as URLs, servers, domains and hyperlinks. But don't be put off. This book will show you that behind all the buzz words, the Internet is fairly simple to understand – and tremendously useful.

This is one of hundreds of maps that you can download from the Internet.

Online galleries and museums are good for images and information.

Information sources

The vast amount of information on the Internet gives you access to encyclopedias, dictionaries, maps, news, magazines, museums and art galleries, articles, and specialist pieces of research. The vital information that you could use in your homework projects is all just a few clicks of your mouse button away. All you have to do is find it. This book will show you how.

Goods and services

You can use the Internet to gain access to all sorts of services. This includes sites that offer a range of things to buy, from books that help you do your homework, to free-to-use information on university courses and careers. You can also find sites that contain galleries of images, which you can use to illustrate your work.

On shopping sites you click on things you want, and a list is stored until you are ready to buy. You can click on a logo like the one below to see what is in your virtual "shopping basket".

Extra programs

You can download all sorts of useful computer programs from the Internet, many of which are free. There are programs that will help you view the Internet more efficiently, and ones that allow you to view documents that have been made in certain formats.

There are also types of programs, called compression software, that enable you to make files smaller. These are really useful when you want to send your files over the Internet, or transfer them onto floppy disks.

WinZip® software is ideal for making your files smaller, so that you can send them quickly via the Internet.

This is the symbol for Real®, the company that makes RealPlayer® – software that speeds up the rate at which you can watch video clips on the Internet.

Communication

The Internet is a fantastic way to send and share information with other homeworkers, no matter where they are in the world. Facilities for this include e-mail, chat rooms on education sites, and message boards. They're a great way to swap information for homework projects, or ask questions of people who have special knowledge of particular subjects. You can also use the Internet to send your homework from computer to computer, so that you may not need to carry it between home and school.

Pictures

Any picture that you see on the Internet can be downloaded and stored on your computer. This means that you could put them into your homework to make your projects more informative, and attractive too. Most organizations that publish on the Internet don't mind if you use their pictures for personal projects – including homework.

Like all publishers, Web sites are protected by the law of copyright, which restricts the use of their words and pictures by other people. Always check the terms and conditions of a Web site before you use any pictures. See "Legal stuff" on page 35 for details.

Here are just a few of the pictures that you can download from the Internet.

How the Internet really works

The Internet is a gigantic computer network. A network is a group of computers that are linked together so that information and resources can be shared between them.

A simple network

At its simplest, a computer network consists of computers that are joined together by cables. Information can pass from computer to computer along the cables.

Information passes around the network along cables.

A more complex network

A network with lots of users accessing the same information has a powerful computer at its heart, called a server. Servers store, sort and distribute information. Other computers on the network, called clients, request, receive and use the information that is stored on the server.

Client computers

Server computer

Information passes from computer to computer via a server, along cables.

The Internet

The Internet is a network of thousands of smaller, separate networks. Server computers are used to dish out information to clients. There are thousands of Internet servers around the world, all fulfilling requests for information, 24 hours a day.

Connecting the networks

The computer networks that make up the Internet are linked together by the telephone systems that you use for ordinary phone calls. These systems consist of cables ranging from old-fashioned copper phone cables to modern, fibre-optic cables made of thin glass strands. These can carry more information than copper cables. Networks are also linked by satellite, microwaves, radio waves and infra-red waves.

Internet service providers

Companies called Internet service providers (ISPs) enable computer users to access the Internet. They own server computers, which process and supply information that is on the Internet.

Router computers

Routers are computers that sort and send information to and from the places where it is stored, along the fastest available path. They are owned by telecommunications companies, network providers, and ISPs.

This picture shows how information moves around the world on the Internet.

Finding a route

When you type in a Web site's address, your computer sends a message via the phone system ① to the ISP with which you are registered.

The ISP's router chooses the quickest route to send the request on to its destination, shown by the red lines ②. The router then sends the message, which goes along the chosen path to another router, then another, then another, and so on. Within seconds, the request is delivered to the server which holds the required information ③. It's called the host server. This is because it hosts information that people can look at.

Within a flash, the server fires the correct file back to your computer. It comes back to you, via routers, along the fastest available channels, shown in blue ④, that are available at the time – just as happened to the original request.

Finally, the information is sent to your computer by your ISP ⑤. All this happens far faster than the time it took you to read this – even if the information is located on the other side of the world.

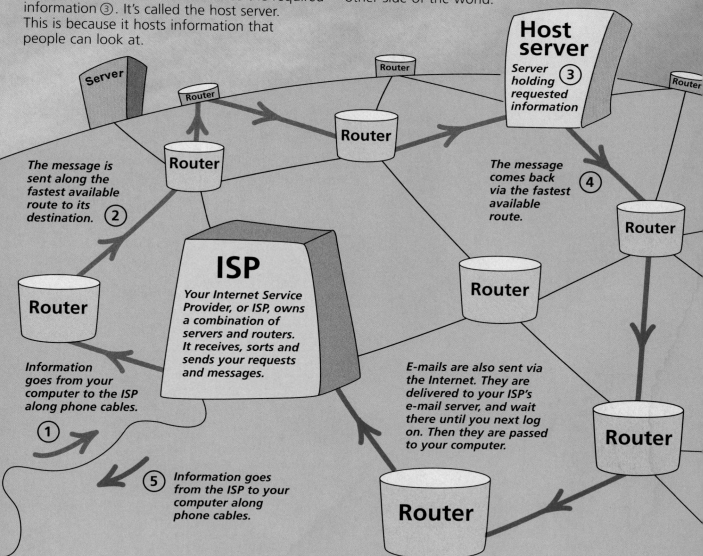

Host server
Server holding ③ requested information

Router

Router

Server

Router

Router

Router

The message is sent along the fastest available route to its destination. ②

The message comes back via the fastest available route. ④

Router

ISP
Your Internet Service Provider, or ISP, owns a combination of servers and routers. It receives, sorts and sends your requests and messages.

Router

Router

Information goes from your computer to the ISP along phone cables. ①

E-mails are also sent via the Internet. They are delivered to your ISP's e-mail server, and wait there until you next log on. Then they are passed to your computer.

Router

Router

⑤ Information goes from the ISP to your computer along phone cables.

What is the World Wide Web?

The World Wide Web, or Web for short, is part of the Internet where you'll find almost all of the interesting, useful and exciting stuff – including homework information. The Web is not a place, as such. It is made up of thousands of Internet servers, which store and send out Web pages.

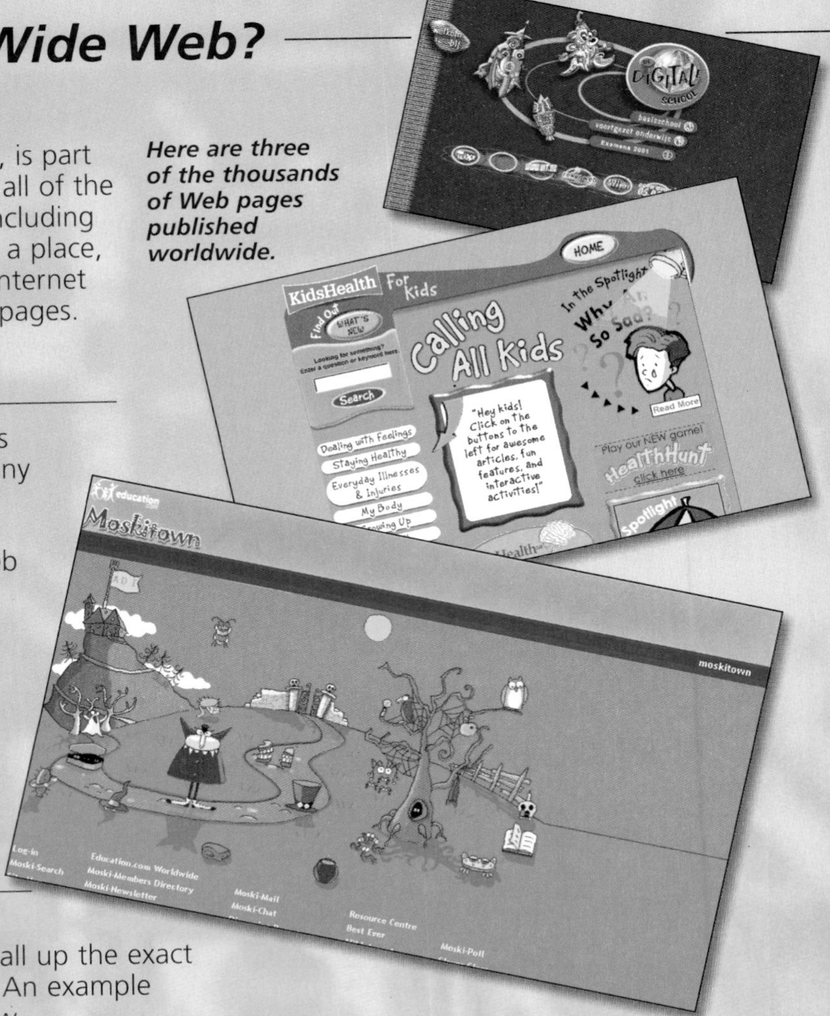

Here are three of the thousands of Web pages published worldwide.

Web sites

A Web site is a collection of Web pages published by a single individual, company or organization. The easiest way to recognize one is by its address, which will most likely begin with *www*. A Web site address is called a URL, short for Uniform Resource Locator.

Information on the Web is displayed on sets of individually designed screens (the Web pages) like the ones shown on the right.

How URLs work

Every single Web page has its own unique URL. A URL enables you to call up the exact page of information that you want. An example of a URL is shown in the panel below.

http://www.homeworkplanet.com/cool.html

This is the protocol name, in other words the code, or format, in which the message is sent. *http* stands for hypertext transfer protocol.

This is the domain name. It identifies the name of the site, but to the Web's routers and servers it stands for a set of numbers, called the Internet Protocol (IP) address. Think of it as working like a type of telephone number, which enables computers to identify and pass on messages to their correct destination. The example above is for a popular homework help site based in the USA.

The file name. This is the name of the file in which the page is stored. The *.html* part shows that the file is written in a particular code, called HyperText Markup Language, or HTML for short. You will see both *.htm* and *.html* used to identify HTML files.

Web browsers

The best way to find and view Web sites is with a Web browser. This is a computer program that is specifically written to find and display Web pages. Today, most computers are supplied with inbuilt Web browsers. The most common one is Microsoft® Internet Explorer. This comes loaded on just about all machines that run the Microsoft Windows® operating systems. This book will show you how to use Internet Explorer.

Click this icon on your desktop to open Internet Explorer.

Home pages

When you go onto a Web site the first page you see is the home page. This is a kind of introductory page. Think of it as being like the front cover of a magazine. It might list the contents of the site, or tell you the latest news about the site or whoever has published it.

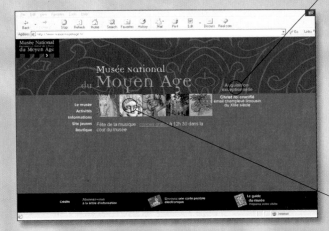

This is the home page of the National Museum of the Middle Ages, in France.

One of the clever things about Web sites is that their pages can be linked to other pages, either within the site or on entirely different sites, by things called hyperlinks. These are words, phrases or pictures that, when clicked on, whizz you instantly to a page that has related information for you to use.

All about hyperlinks

Text hyperlinks are usually displayed in a different shade from the rest of the text. They may also be underlined. When you move your mouse pointer over a hyperlink, the pointer icon will turn into a pointing hand.

The hand icon

This page was displayed by clicking on a hyperlink in some text on the Web page shown on the left.

Picture hyperlinks don't look any different from regular pictures. However, as with text hyperlinks, when you move your mouse pointer over them, the pointer icon becomes a pointing hand.

This page appeared after clicking on a picture hyperlink.

Clicking on the picture instructs the Web browser to call up the linked page. This then appears in the browser in place of the page you were looking at previously.

Browsing basics

At first, the Internet can be a confusing place to get around. But the World Wide Web and your browser enable you to explore it without getting lost. The guide on these pages will help you get to know Microsoft® Internet Explorer, the most widely used of all browsers.

The logo for Microsoft Internet Explorer 6 is shown below. If you don't have it already, you can download it for free from Microsoft's Web site.

Using Microsoft Internet Explorer

You can go to any Web site simply by typing its URL in the **Address** box at the top of Internet Explorer's window. To get used to using the browser, try exploring a Web site, such as the site for Usborne Publishing. Type the URL shown below in the **Address** box, then press **Enter**.

Address 🗐 http://www.usborne.com

The home page will start to appear in your browser's window. The page builds up as pictures and text are copied from the host Web server to your computer's memory. This process is called downloading. Most Web pages don't take much longer than a few seconds to download.

Following links

Once you have opened a home page, try following some hyperlinks to see what further information you can find. You could try this with the Usborne Web site, for example.

Using your mouse, start by moving the pointer around, noticing where it changes into a pointing hand. Each time it does, your cursor is going over a hyperlink. Click on one of them, using your left-hand mouse button, and your browser will display the hyperlinked page.

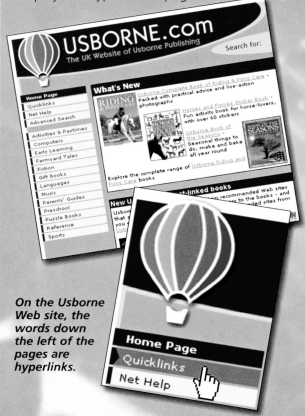

On the Usborne Web site, the words down the left of the pages are hyperlinks.

When you are on the new page, click on another hyperlink. Repeat this step as often as you like. Don't worry about getting lost – in the next section we'll show you how to retrace your steps.

Going back

To go back to the previous Web page that you looked at, simply click on your browser's **Back** button. Look for the logo shown on the left – it's in the top left-hand corner of the browser. Click on it and the previous page will appear almost immediately.

Going forward again

If you decide that you would like to re-view pages that you looked at before you clicked on the Back button, press the **Forward** button – it is just to the right of the Back button. You can go back and forward as often as you like.

Stop

If a Web page is taking too long to download, or if, while it is still downloading, you decide that you don't want to look at it after all, press the **Stop** button. This will tell the browser to stop accepting files from the URL that is downloading.

Refresh

If you would like to check that you are looking at the latest version of a particular Web page, or if some parts of the page did not download at the last attempt, click on the **Refresh** button.

Home

Whenever Internet Explorer opens it will go to a particular Web page, which you can set for yourself – turn to page 62, "Setting your start page", to find out how. Whenever you want to go back to this page, simply click on the **Home** button.

Storing and organizing Web pages

Microsoft® Internet Explorer remembers Web pages that it has visited and displays them if you press on the button marked **History**. This enables you to gain quick access to the homework sites that you've used in the past. You can also save and organize useful Web pages into a folder called **Favorites**.

Know your history

With Internet Explorer, "History" refers to the record of Web pages that the browser stores when it has visited them.

① To view the record, start by clicking on the **History** button at the top of the browser.

② A list appears on the screen, giving names of sites that have been visited. Go down the list until you see a Web site that you want to look at.

③ Click on the site. A list of all the site's pages that you visited will appear. Click once with your mouse on the page that you want and the browser will open the selected Web page.

④ There are different ways that you can display the History list. Choose the one that you find most useful. To do this, click **View**. A menu drops down. Make your choice and the selection will automatically be re-ordered.

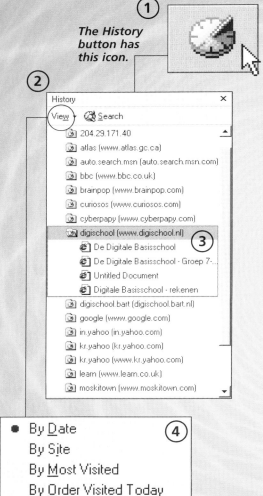

The History button has this icon.

Typing this asks your browser to search for URLs that include this name.

History search

To search for a Web site within the History folder, click on **Search**. Then enter the address, or as much of it as you can remember, or even just a word from it, and press **OK**. Internet Explorer will then trawl through its History, and show a list of Web pages that contain the words you asked for.

The settings for how many sites are stored in the History folder can be altered. To find out how to do this, see page 62.

Favorites button

The **Favorites** button enables you to save Web page addresses in a folder. You'll find it at the top of the Internet Explorer browser. Click on it and a list will appear at the left of the browser. Internet Explorer comes with a few sites already stored in the Favorites folder.

Add a new Favorite

To add a new page to your Favorites list, click **Add...** and a new window will open, entitled **Add Favorite**.

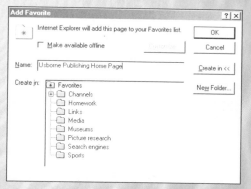

This is the icon that appears on the Add... button.

A description of the Web page open at the time will be displayed in a little window called **Name**. Click **OK** and the Web page will be added to your list of Favorites.

Tip

Sometimes, the description of a Web site in the Favorites folder may be a little too long-winded, or too brief, for your liking. You can change the description before you add the site to your Favorites list, simply by editing the description that appears in the Name box, before you press OK.

Organizing Favorites

The list of Favorites can become pretty chaotic, so it is a good idea to organize it into separate, themed folders. That way, you can keep particular types of Web pages together.

To organize your Favorites, open the Favorites window and then click on **Organize...**

This icon is on the Organize... button.

You now have four options, shown below. Click on **Create Folder** to make a new folder. This new folder, which you can name, will now appear in the list.

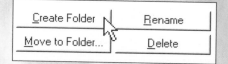

To put a file into the folder that you just created, first click on the file that you want to move. Now click on **Move to Folder**. A window called **Browse for Folder** will appear. Highlight the folder that you wish to use, then click **OK**. The file will now be saved into that folder.

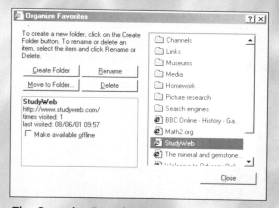

The Organize Favorites window

Downloading programs

There are lots of computer programs available on the Internet which you can download and use to help you with your homework. Many of them won't cost you anything.

Useful downloads

The most useful downloads are those that enable you to view and use documents that you are likely to find on the Web. One example of this is the widely used Adobe® Acrobat® Reader, which enables you to look at documents that have been converted to Adobe's Portable Document Format (PDF).

The box below has details of some useful programs and links to the sites where you can find them. Many of these are "plug-ins". These enable you to use documents that have been made using a particular type of software.

Internet links

For links to all the sites mentioned here, go to **www.usborne-quicklinks.com** and type the keyword **homework**.

Useful downloads

Adobe® Acrobat® Reader Enables you to view files created in the Portable Document Format (PDF). This format is particularly useful because it has the effect of compressing large and complicated files, so that they transmit quickly via the Internet.

Macromedia® Shockwave® Enables your browser to view the many Web sites that use animated features which have been created using Shockwave software.

Quicktime® Enables your browser to play video, sound and 3-D "virtual reality" scenes sent via the Internet.

RealPlayer™ Enables you to watch and listen to video and audio files without first having to load them onto your computer's hard disk. This speeds up the rate at which you can watch video and listen to sounds. Look for the **RealPlayer Basic** hyperlink, to download the basic, free version.

These Web sites contain links to lots of downloads

TuKids For child-friendly downloads, including fun-to-use learning software, and much more.

Kids' Domain Downloads Contains excellent educational programs to help you with your studies.

How to download

Once you have found a file that you would like to download, follow these steps.

1. Click on the hyperlink that starts the download. It may be an icon, a word or phrase, such as "Download Now", or maybe even the title of the document.

2. A box will appear, entitled **File Download**, confirming what you have chosen to do, and giving you details of which Web server the file you want to download is located on. To start the download, choose **Save this file to disk** and then click the **OK** button.

3. Another box will appear, entitled **Save As**. This enables you to choose where you wish to store your file.
If you are in doubt about where to store the file, click on the **Create New Folder** icon shown here and create a folder for it to go in. When you are ready to begin the download, click **Save**.

The Create New Folder icon

4 While the file is downloading, a progress box will appear, telling you things such as how much of the file has been downloaded, and the speed of transfer.

Be patient, things can go slowly at this point. Don't turn off your computer, or your connection to the Internet at this stage – you will spoil the download.

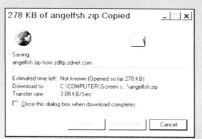

Progress box

278 KB of angelfsh.zip Copied

Saving:
angelfsh.zip from zdftp.zdnet.com

Estimated time left: Not known (Opened so far 278 KB)
Download to: C:\COMPUTER\Screen s...\angelfsh.zip
Transfer rate: 3.05 KB/Sec

☐ Close this dialog box when download completes

5 When the download is complete, the icon shown on the right will appear in the progress box. You will then have the option to **Open** the downloaded folder, so that the program will work on your computer.

"Download complete" icon

You may be led through a step-by-step procedure.

6 You might find that the downloaded file is held in, say, a WinZip® compression folder (see page 51). If this is the case, when you open the WinZip folder, look for the file that has the icon shown above next to it.

Click to decompress

Double-click on this icon and the program will decompress itself. Then you will be able to use it in the same way as any other program on your computer.

These logos show just a few of the really useful sources of downloads that are available on the Internet.

Search and find

The Internet has no particular order of its own. It's a little like a library that contains millions of books, but nobody has put them in order. Looking for things in all that chaos can be frustrating, unless you get someone else to do it for you. And that's exactly what services such as directories and indexes, often called search engines, will do. They hunt through the mess of the Internet and World Wide Web to find you the documents you ask for. And what's more... they're free.

Directories

Web directories are run by organizations which collect information about Web sites and arrange them in categories and sub-categories. Categories are connected by hyperlinks, so that you can make your search more and more precise until you have a short list of relevant sites.

Yahoo! is a directory-type search engine. An example of how you might use it to find exactly what you want is shown here. In the example, imagine that you want to find out about Giraffes.

1. First, go to the **Science** section and click on **Animals**. This will download a page with a number of headings.

2. Click on **Mammals**, and you will download another page with a list of mammals.

3. Click on **Giraffes** to download a list of sites devoted to giraffes.

4. Choose the site that you want to look at.

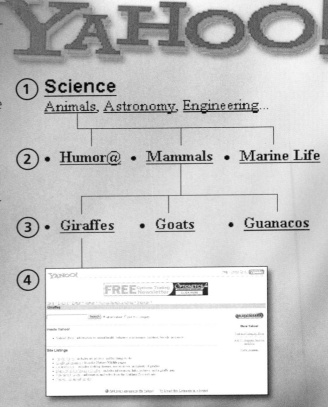

Searching Yahoo!

If you are not sure which category to look under, try typing a word or phrase in the Search box at the top of the page. For example, if you want to find out all about volcanoes, type **volcanoes** in the Search box. Yahoo! will look for any news articles, categories in its own directory and links to Web sites that relate to this subject, and display a selection of results.

If you want to make the search more precise, type words related to your search subject in the Search box. For example, if you want to find out about the eruption of the volcano Mount Vesuvius in AD63 try typing **Vesuvius AD63**. Yahoo! will look for documents that contain both terms.

Google™

Indexes

Indexes are search engines that explore the Web, finding new sites and adding them to their own huge list of pages. When you use an index, it will scan the list for words matching your search and show you a number of results, or "hits", in order of how closely they appear to match your needs.

For example, if you want to find out about tropical storms, type **tropical storms** in the Search box, and click on **Search**. An example of a search, and its results, are shown in the two pictures below.

You type what you want to search for here.

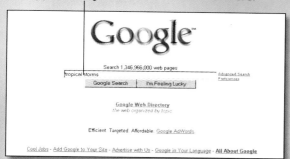

Index results

Each item in an index's list of results has a hyperlink to a Web page, plus a little information about the page. The first few entries in the results list are likely to match your search closely, but lower down the list the links are less likely to be relevant.

Pages 20-23 have more information about how to get the best results from search engines.

These are the first few results of a search.

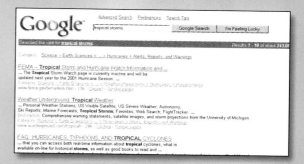

Combination searches

AltaVista® is an example of a search engine that lets you look for things in several different ways. It has directories and indexes that you can use, and options that allow you to search for things more rapidly, or in greater depth than normal.

Internet links

For links to all these sites, go to **www.usborne-quicklinks.com** and type the keyword **homework**.

AltaVista®   **Google®**   **Yahoo!®**

Be safe

Search engines automatically find any matches that seem relevant to your searches. However, sometimes this means that they find offensive material. To cut down on these irrelevant results, choose your search words as carefully as you can. When results come back, read the short description of a site before you open it, to make sure that it is relevant.

Many search engines now offer "safe search" or "family friendly" options where you can customize the search engine to block offensive material. Look for links called "Customize" or "Safe search" on the search engine's home page.

Metasearchers

In the world of computers, the word *meta* means "about". Metasearchers are a type of search engine that automatically search other search engines to find results to your initial query. They give you a selection of the best results from each search engine they consult – which can save you time.

Ask Jeeves is available in Spanish and English.

Do you have a question?

Ask Jeeves® is a metasearcher that lets you phrase searches as questions.

Once you ask Jeeves a question, descriptions of the Web pages that most closely answer your question will be shown. Chances are, one will have the exact answer to your question.

With Ask Jeeves, you can choose to look at questions asked by other users about particular subjects. You can also view questions being asked by other users, to give you an idea how to phrase your queries.

Tip

Although metasearchers will give you many useful results, you might sometimes find that they return things that are a bit of a waste of your time, from a homework point of view. For more focused results, you might prefer to use metasearchers specifically designed for kids. See page 23 for details.

Metasearch software

There is a range of metasearch software that you can download from the Internet. You can use it to help you trawl the Web more quickly and thoroughly than ever before.

Try them out

The price of metasearch software varies – some is even available, with limited features, for free. Many of the programs allow you to use trial versions for several days to see whether you like them, and how useful you find them, before you buy.

Things to look for...

- Software that gives you control over the number of results produced per search.
- Helpful descriptions of each site found.
- Adjustable settings so that you can filter out unsuitable material.
- The ability to search a good number of high-quality search engines.

Things to avoid...

- Software that is always slow.
- Metasearchers that, quite simply, you find annoying to use.
- Software that cannot be adjusted to suit your needs.
- Overcomplicated software. It will slow down your searching, and take you longer to get used to. The more features a metasearcher has, the more likely it is to do this.

WebFerret

WebFerret™ can be downloaded from the Internet. The free version searches through up to 21 different search engines, directories and indexes. It is very simple to use, and it can also be adapted to suit your needs.

You can alter WebFerret's settings, including the list of search engines that it consults and the number of results that it brings back to you. To start doing this, click on **View**, then choose **Options**. Make your choices under the options **Search Engines** and **Advanced**.

Bingooo

Bingooo® is a metasearching browser that you can download for free. It provides you with information about the sites that it finds. It searches several sources at the same time and brings you results very quickly.

You can specify the type of information you want by choosing from a list at the left of the Bingooo browser. For example, you can set it to search only for images, or to hunt for encyclopedia articles about your chosen subject.

When it displays its results, Bingooo highlights the word or phrase that you used in your search.

Copernic

A basic, but still powerful, version of the metasearcher Copernic® is available for free. To download it, click on Downloads, choose Copernic Basic, and then follow the online instructions. With a standard modem it can take up to 20 minutes to download, so be patient.

Copernic installs a browser to your computer. To search for something, simply type the words that you want into the **Quick search** box, then hit the arrow symbol to its right. While the search is conducted, a display shows the progress made with its inquiries of various search engines.

Copernic is available in several languages.

Another tip

Metasearchers will find a wide selection of material which, unfortunately, might include things that you will find offensive. To cut down the risk of this, check your metasearcher's instructions to find out how to set its filters. Also, set Microsoft® Internet Explorer to filter unwanted material (see page 56).

Internet links – metasearchers

For links to all these sites, go to *www.usborne-quicklinks.com* and type the keyword **homework**.

Ask Jeeves® Phrase your search as a question.

Bingooo® If you can speak German then you may also find the German-language version of this metasearcher useful.

Ithaki Available in many languages. Also has an option that enables you to search only children's search engines.

Copernic® Different versions are available to download. You'll need to pay for the most powerful one.

WebFerret™ The pay-for version conducts powerful searches. The free version is quick to download.

Top search tips

When you're searching for homework information, speed is of the essence. You're not just surfing the Internet for fun – you want quick results. Here are some tips to get you started.

Make a search engine your start page

If you find that you like using a particular search engine, you could make it into the page that opens up when you go on the Internet. That way, you can start searching from the moment that you go online. To find out how to do this, see page 62.

Within seconds of opening the browser, a search on the topic "solar system" yielded all these results.

Ten top tips

- Read the search engine's instructions. Look for a hyperlink on the search engine's home page that says "Help", or something else that suggests a source of instructions.

- If you're not exactly sure which keywords to type in, try consulting a directory (see page 16). Click on a keyword that looks the most helpful to you, and then narrow down your search. Soon, you should arrive at a list of useful sites.

- If you find that you're not getting the results that you want from a search, try using a different search engine.

- Keep your searches simple. Don't clutter up a search with unnecessary words.

explanation of centrifugal force	Search

An overcomplicated search

centrifugal force	Search

A well-defined search

- If you want to find information about several related things, try to think of a phrase that links them together, then search for that.

ducks pigs sheep cows hens	Search

This search will yield disappointing results.

farm animals	Search

This search is more likely to be successful.

- Check your spelling when you enter words into a search engine. Your search engine will look for exactly what you typed in.

astromony	Search

The query returned no results; please try another query

astronomy	Search

Web Pages: 108,690 pages found.

- Search results can offer up Web sites that look interesting, but have little to do with what you may be looking for. Many search engines display a brief description of each Web site. Check the description carefully before you decide whether it's relevant.

dinosaurs	Search

cuddly fluffy dinosaur babies for you to collect and love and cherish and hug and kiss.....
http://www.diniwini.com

Probably irrelevant

dinosaurs	Search

pictures and information on prehistoric animals from the Triassic, Jurassic, and Cretaceous eras....
http://www.mondodinosaur.com

Probably relevant

- Be as specific as you can.

respiration	Search

Web Pages: 108,690 pages found.

Not specific enough – too many results.

plant respiration	Search

Web Pages: 181 pages found.

Just right. Many of these results will be relevant.

- Don't be too impatient. If you don't get the result you want first time around, perhaps you're just not using the correct words in your search. Maybe you should think again.

- Remember that the Internet isn't the only source of information. Try libraries, encyclopedias, or other reference books. They might even help you find a better term to put into the search engines.

Smart searching

Here are some handy, easy-to-use skills that will bring your searching up to the highest level.

Make use of "operators"

Shorthand instructions, called operators, make your search more specific. Different search engines use different operators, so for best results, look at the tips available on each one before you begin using them. Most search engines recognize two operators: **+** and **–**.

+ stands for *and*. If you want to search for sites that include all of your keywords, rather than just any of them, type **+** before each word in the Search box. So, if you want to find out about balloons, but are more interested in airships than party balloons, type **+balloons +airships** in the Search box. The search engine will only find pages which include both terms.

+balloons +airships	Search

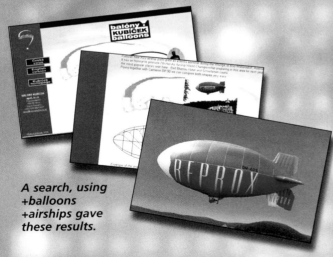

A search, using +balloons +airships gave these results.

– stands for *not*. You can exclude terms by typing a **–** sign before a word. For example, if you are looking for the history of Rome, but not Ancient Rome, you could type **+Rome +history –ancient**.

+rome +history -ancient	Search

Try quotation marks

If you want to base your search on a particular phrase, try putting that phrase inside quotation marks. Say, for example, you want to find information for a project on space stations. Put the words in quotation marks, so that you enter **"space station"**, and you will only get results that mention space stations as opposed to any other type of station, or anything else to do with space.

"space station"	Search

A search that specified "space station" gave these results.

Beware of capital letters

If you use capital letters, as in **+Ancient +History**, most search engines will only find pages which use capital letters in the same places. If you don't include capitals, as in **+ancient +history**, your results will include pages whether they use capitals or not.

Use search engines for kids

There are a number of search engines that are specially designed for use by young people. They list things that are particularly suited to younger Web surfers, meaning that you will quickly find sites that are tailored to your homework needs. Use these for your searching and you won't need to wade through all those irrelevant sites.

This man has the answer.

Ask Jeeves Kids
This is the children's version of the metasearcher Ask Jeeves®. Ask a question, and Jeeves will come up with a list of sites that are likely to have the answer. Jeeves will also direct you to other metasearchers, which may be able to answer your query.

Some kids' search engines are free. Others, like Surf Monkey, charge a small subscription.

KidsClick!
This educational directory is run by librarians, so it is thorough, and leads you to a variety of reliable resources. It is arranged in two ways: according to subject categories, and also alphabetically. You can search using keywords, or view documents according to particular subject matters.

Indexplorian is an educational search engine for French and Dutch speakers.

Education World
This American Web site was originally made for teachers. It lists only educational Web sites, making it a great resource for students to search as well. Your searches should yield a very useful list of relevant Web sites.

Milkmoon provides searches for German speakers.

CyberSleuth Kids
This is a directory of hundreds of sites, aimed at students, which can be searched, or browsed in school subject categories. It has some very good links to clipart Web sites. (For more about clipart, see pages 36-37.)

Yahooligans!
This is the junior version of Yahoo! You can search the entire index, or focus your search first by choosing a category to look through.

Internet links

For links to all these sites, go to *www.usborne-quicklinks.com* and type the keyword **homework**.

Ask Jeeves Kids℠	KidsClick!
CyberSleuth Kids	SurfMonkey™
Education World®	Yahooligans!®
Ithaki for Kids	

What are education Web sites?

Education Web sites are usually large, with lots of useful resources for different school stages and subjects, and teachers too. Many of the sites include tests, study aids, chat rooms, facilities where you can question experts, and even dictionaries – in case you're ever stuck for words.

I may be able to help.

Some education sites contain a directory of links to other sites, too. These features are all described on the next few pages.

Ages and stages

Some education sites are designed with only one age group in mind. Many allow you to choose your age or school stage before you begin your research. That way, the information you find will be suitable for your educational level.

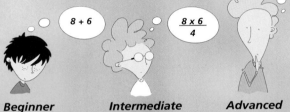

$8 + 6$ $\dfrac{8 \times 6}{4}$ $\dfrac{8^n \times 6^{2n+1}}{4^{n-1}}$

Beginner   **Intermediate**   **Advanced**

What's on them?

The content of education sites varies, but most contain questions and answers, fact sheets, lessons, links to other sites and study tips. Many have puzzles, games, quizzes and other interactive features too.

Some education sites act as stepping-stones to other useful sites on the Web, whereas others are entirely self-contained information sources. If you are researching homework or a project, they can provide the information you need.

Examples of education sites from around the world

Built-in searches

Almost all education sites have a built-in search engine. Entering a keyword will generate a list of responses, which may refer to a collection of questions, answers and facts on that site, or give links to other sites on the subject. Some education sites find and review useful Web sites and organize them into searchable categories.

Homework help

Homework help sites are designed specifically to help with assignments and projects. They usually allow you to send in questions, which an expert will answer for you. There are also archives of past questions and answers, so you can see if your question has been answered before. For more information, see page 31.

Here are three of the best ways to find information from a homework help site:

- Ask a question. An expert will answer it.

> *Can penguins fly?*

- Check the archive. It shows all previously asked questions, with experts' answers.

> *Q: Do penguins have wings?*
>
> *A: Yes, but they cannot fly. Their wings are adapted so that they are powerful swimmers. They use their wings like flippers.*

- Follow the Web site's suggested links to good sources of information.

> *Click here to go to PBS Life of Birds Web site.*
>
> *Click here to go to the BBC's live Birdcam.*

Reference sites

The Web is a great source of general reference tools to use when you're researching a subject. Some education sites have built-in reference areas, but most link to external sites, such as those described below. Find out more on pages 28-29.

Dictionaries These allow you to find the meaning of a word by typing it into a search box. Many have extra features, such as pronunciation guides and translations into foreign languages.

Dicorama.com

Dicorama is a French dictionary that translates.

Encyclopedias These offer a good introduction to almost any subject. Online encyclopedias often include built-in hyperlinks to other related topics and Web sites, if you want further information.

Encarta

Microsoft® Encarta® encyclopedia is available in English, French, German, Italian and Spanish.

Atlases These allow you to search quickly for maps of a particular country or region. They usually provide extra facts and figures on historical background, population and culture.

This site, at atlas.gc.ca has detailed maps of Canada.

Almanacs These are similar to encyclopedias but often have articles which focus on a particular range of topics in more depth. They are a good source of up-to-date facts and figures.

Try them out

Some education sites are more detailed, or more varied, or easier to use than others. When you first start using them, visit a good selection, to give you a good idea of what they all offer.

On many education sites, the information is arranged and presented so that it tallies with a particular education system – usually that of the site's home country. To compare different education systems, and the way that they describe different educational levels, go to *www.usborne-quicklinks.com* and type the keyword **homework**. There, you'll find an easy-to-use comparison chart. Follow it and you'll soon be able to use Web sites that are written according to different education systems.

How accurate are they?

Education sites are generally written by experts, so the information they provide should be accurate. However, if you're not sure about the accuracy of any information you find, try to double-check it against other sources, such as a book, a CD-ROM or a good online encyclopedia, such as Britannica.

Britannica is a popular English-language encyclopedia.

Fact Monster is a Web site that contains an encyclopedia, an almanac, a dictionary and an atlas.

Chat and messages

Chatting on the Internet means having a live, written conversation with one or more people at the same time. Messages can also be put onto the Internet for a number of people to respond to later, using facilities called messsage boards or forums.

Educational chat rooms

Many education sites have chat rooms that allow you to talk about educational topics. This is a great way to ask specific questions and get information quickly from students, teachers or subject experts, for your homework. Look for "Chat", "Messages" or "Forum" headings on the home pages of sites that you use.

In general, you must be wary about using chat rooms. They can be used by people who simply want to be offensive or to harrass. Chat rooms on education sites are monitored, so you should be able to use them without being hassled.

Special guests

Sometimes, experts in a subject are invited into chat rooms, and you can ask them questions about their area of study. Sites usually have an "events calendar" showing when guests will visit. Many also offer transcripts of past chat sessions.

Getting started

Before you enter a chat room, you'll almost always need to provide a name, and sometimes a password. This is so other users can recognize you, and so the site owners know who is using the chat room. Despite the fact that education site chat rooms are monitored, you should not give out personal information. To do so is, potentially, to put your own safety at risk.

User Name: Bubble

Think of a name you will be able to remember. It can be whatever you like.

Inside a chat room

Once you have entered your chosen nickname and password, you'll be allowed into the chat room. A list of other users will appear on the side of the screen ①, so you can instantly tell who else is there.

An example of a homework chat room Web site

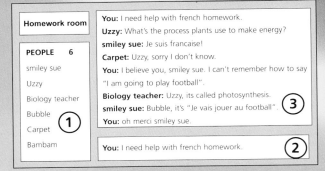

Homework room	
PEOPLE 6	**You:** I need help with french homework.
smiley sue	**Uzzy:** What's the process plants use to make energy?
Uzzy	**smiley sue:** Je suis francaise!
Biology teacher	**Carpet:** Uzzy, sorry I don't know.
Bubble	**You:** I believe you, smiley sue. I can't remember how to say "I am going to play football".
Carpet ①	**Biology teacher:** Uzzy, its called photosynthesis.
Bambam	**smiley sue:** Bubble, it's "Je vais jouer au football". ③
	You: oh merci smiley sue.

You: I need help with french homework. ②

To chat, you enter text into a box at the bottom of the screen ②. This then appears in the main window ③ and can be read by all the other users. If you want to chat with a particular person, remember to put their name in your message so they know you're talking to them. There may be more than one conversation going on at a time.

When you've finished chatting, press the "Log off" or "Exit" button. This should automatically take you out of the chat room.

Tip

Some sites have a number of chat rooms each of which deal with a different topic. It's a good idea to join only one at a time, though, as it's tricky to hold lots of conversations at once!

Dos and Don'ts

Do use the site's search box first if you're looking for the answer to a homework query. You might find it's already been answered in a previous chat session, or elsewhere on the site.

Do find out if the chat room has an FAQ (Frequently Asked Questions), and read it before you enter. They're the best guides to what you should and shouldn't say or do.

Do plan what you want to say, and be as clear and concise as possible. Lts of baddly rittn txt cn B frstr8ng 2 rd!

Don't rush into talking in a chat room. A good way to start is by "lurking", that is, just reading what's going on.

Don't type in capital letters. This is the text equivalent of SHOUTING!

Don't be rude or abusive if someone says something you disagree with. This is called "flaming" and it is likely to get you thrown out of a monitored chat room.

⚠ Be safe

There is a real risk that people who take an unhealthy sexual interest in young people may visit chat rooms, posing as fellow students. If you're in a chat room and someone says something creepy:

- **Don't reply.**
- **Report the incident** to the host site's managers – there should be an e-mail link on the site that enables you to do this.
- **Never, ever give personal information**, such as your full name and home address or your school's name and address.
- **See page 57 for fuller details.**

Message boards and messages

A few sites have message boards, or forums. Here, you can leave questions and comments of your own, or reply to someone else's. You can't chat directly with someone on a board, but it does allow you to share a query with many people.

An example of message board subjects

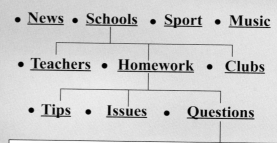

- **News** • **Schools** • **Sport** • **Music**
- **Teachers** • **Homework** • **Clubs**
- **Tips** • **Issues** • **Questions**

Bubble: *Does anyone know a good science museum Web site?*

Scotch Mysty: *I like the Franklin Institute best, it has cool dinosaur bits.*

Ben: *Bubble, try exploratorium.*

> **REPLY**

REPLY: Add your own message to the board

There can be dozens of replies to a single query (or "post"). You may get good information quickly... but be warned, replies may just be people's opinions, and are not necessarily correct. It's important that you check things with a source that you know gives good information, such as trusted Web sites, or encyclopedias.

Personal information

As with educational chat rooms, it is important that you don't give out personal information when you use, or register for, message boards. It's all too easy for people to access your details this way.

Online encyclopedias and dictionaries

An encyclopedia is a reliable reference source which gives summarized information about different topics. It won't tell you as much about a subject as a specialized Web site will, but it should provide a good starting point for your homework research, presenting all the key facts you will need to know. You can use these as the basis for further searching, which should flesh out your basic information.

Searching an online encyclopedia

Online encyclopedias usually work in a similar way to search engines (see pages 16-17). The type of results you get will depend on the encyclopedia. Most will return a main entry and a selection of additional entries that relate closely to that topic. For example, if you typed in "Van Gogh", the main entry would probably provide a biography, and details of his famous works. Extra entries might offer information on other painting styles or artists of the same era.

These are various encyclopedia results from the search "Van Gogh".

Using links

Sometimes, main encyclopedia articles also contain hyperlinks that will take you to another relevant article in the encyclopedia, for example:

> "Dutch painter, generally considered the greatest after Rembrandt, and one of the greatest of the Post-Impressionists"

These can be a valuable source of extra information, but think carefully about how likely they are to help you before you follow them.

Online encyclopedias such as Britannica and Microsoft® Encarta® also provide links to other sites as well as other Web pages of their own. This can be a convenient way to find out more about a topic without you having to resort to a search engine to find more information.

Some encyclopedias grade each hyperlink to another site according to the site's quality and content.

Rating: ★
Rating: ★★
Rating: ★★★
Rating: ★★★★

Online dictionaries

Online dictionaries help you quickly find the meaning of a word quickly by entering it into a search field. Like a printed dictionary, they offer multiple meanings and information on a word's origin and function, but most offer other features too.

Some dictionaries allow you to listen to the way a word is pronounced. Some will translate words into different languages.

Often, you'll find that an online dictionary will work as a thesaurus. This means that it not only gives the meaning of a word, but also offers similar words and synonyms (words that mean the same thing).

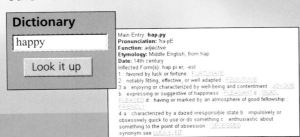

Atlases and maps

You can use an online atlas to search for any country or region, usually by entering its name into a search box or by pointing and clicking on a world map.

Most online atlas sites offer information relating to history, landscape and population as well as geographical and political maps. Some map sites are designed to be used by people who are planning to travel, but they are also useful for students. Good online maps allow you to pinpoint a tiny area of any country, right down to finding the street you live on.

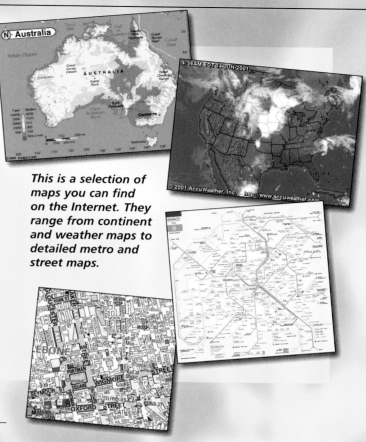

This is a selection of maps you can find on the Internet. They range from continent and weather maps to detailed metro and street maps.

Almanacs

Almanacs are used to find out information which relates to a specific day, month or year. Some contain general information, whereas others focus on a particular topic, such as sport or astronomy.

Many education and reference sites include almanacs, which are updated on a regular (usually daily) basis. They contain features like news, facts and figures, and special reports on different topics. Almanacs are great for finding precise historical facts, such as what important events took place on a specific date.

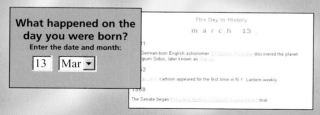

If you enter the year or exact date of your birth into an almanac, you can find out what historical events took place around the world at that time.

Internet links

For links to all these sites, go to *www.usborne-quicklinks.com* and type the keyword **homework**.

Britannica A well-established, authoritative encyclopedia. Has in-depth articles, pictures, and links to other Web sites.

CIA World Factbook Detailed information on just about every country in the world. Ideal for geography projects.

Compton's Encyclopedia Online™ An excellent resource, with articles, maps and pictures covering hundreds of topics.

Infoplease® A trusty almanac, dictionary and encyclopedia, all in one. Also links to *Fact Monster*, a homework-oriented version of Infoplease.

National Geographic maps Includes an online world atlas, printable maps, and lots more.

Microsoft® Encarta® Encyclopedia articles, a world atlas, pictures, maps and links to related Web sites.

Word Central A very good dictionary. Principally uses American English spellings with British English as alternatives.

Wordsmyth™ A useful online thesaurus.

Yahooligans!® Kids Almanac Split into fifteen different categories, to help you find quickly the information that you want.

Homework sites

Homework sites offer reference materials, advice on study, search facilities and expert help, all designed to make doing homework easier and more enjoyable. Information on any school subject is never more than a few clicks away.

A selection of homework help sites available on the Web.

Types of homework sites

The examples shown below explain two of the most common approaches taken by homework sites. Try out the different types for yourself, and see which ones you like best. You'll find a list of recommended sites at *www.usborne-quicklinks.com*.

Subject based

This type of site works like a directory. You select a subject and follow a series of sub-categories until you reach a list of links to sites about your chosen topic.

- **English** • **History** • **Science** • **Music**
- **Biology** • **Zoology** • **Chemistry**

This sort of homework site will offer you a list of Web sites that may be of use.

Animals
Animal search - search for information on a particular animal.
Rainforest animals - all about endangered animals and how you can help them
Insect world - in-depth information on all types of creepy crawlies
Endangered List - an online list of the most endangered animals in the world
Under the sea - amazing photos and information about life under the water.

Question based

Many homework sites allow you to ask questions on various subjects, which will be answered by the site's experts. All the questions, along with their answers, are then compiled into one huge, searchable archive. Before you send in a question, check the site's archive to see if it has been asked before.

how do bees make honey?

If any of the search results look like they might answer your question, take a look at the full answer.

Search results
You searched for: How do bees make honey?
There are **9** relevant questions in the archive.

1. **What do bees eat?** (Sent by Sidney from Sydney.)
Hi Sidney. Well, bees don't eat flowers, that's for sure...

2. **What's a beebole?** (Sent by Lil from Lille.)
Unusual question, Lil. A beebole was what people kept bees in before they invented bee hives...

3. **Can anyone keep bees?** (Sent by Chester from Manchester.)
Hi Chester. I guess it depends on which country you live in. Best to check with...

Tip

Some homework sites are divided into age groups and study levels. Try searching at levels other than your own. Searching at a lower level can be a good way to get a grounding in a subject that you find difficult. Searching at a higher level is a great way to get extra information on a subject, if you need it.

Extra features

A number of homework sites offer both a directory of links and a question and answer service, and many provide more than just information about school subjects. Some give tips on different aspects of school work, such as how to improve your note-taking or give better oral reports. Others have features relating to news or events which change daily, so you'll find new information every time you go there. A few sites can help you study for exams and tests; you can find out more about these on page 33.

Searching the archives

Here are some useful tips on searching question-and-answer archives.

- As with all searches on the Web, try to be as specific as possible. Usually, a single keyword will produce far too many results.

```
insects
```

This search produced 69 results.

```
how bees make honey
```

This search produced just 8 results.

- Don't worry about phrasing your search as a question. The search engine will look for the keywords, not the whole sentence.

- If you type in a phrase, such as

```
19th century poets
```

the highest entries in the list of search results will contain that whole phrase. Lower entries in the list may only contain the words "19th", "century" or "poets", so they are unlikely to be of much use.

> **1. Where can I find out about 19th century poets?**
> (Sent by Byron in Birmingham.)
> You could try your local library. Alternatively, there are Web sites...

> **79. Was life nasty and short in the 19th century?**
> (Sent by Rousseau from Rio.)
> Funny you should ask that, Rousseau...

Result number 1 in the search list will probably match your question closer than a result further down the list.

- If your search produces no hits at all, try other words that are linked to the topic; for instance, if you searched unsuccessfully for "Henry VIII", try "the Tudors" or "British kings".

Asking a question

> So, how *do* bees make honey?

If you are sure that nobody else has asked a question about the topic you're researching, try submitting one yourself. On a typical homework help site, this is how you'd go about it.

(1) Look around the Web site for a hyperlink that invites you to send in a question. Click on the hyperlink and a form will appear.

Ask a question

(2) Complete the form by typing in the question, plus other requested information, such as your name and your question. To finish, click on **Send**.

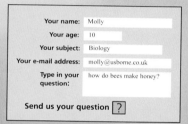

Your name:	Molly
Your age:	10
Your subject:	Biology
Your e-mail address:	molly@usborne.co.uk
Type in your question:	how do bees make honey?

Send us your question [?]

This is an example of the sort of form you will have to fill in when asking a question.

Don't give your full name, just a nickname will be fine.

Obtaining an answer

> Hi Molly,
> Bees collect a substance called nectar from plants. Bees have the ability to turn the sugary nectar into honey as they can

Some homework sites answer all questions via e-mail, while others put the answer on the Web site. You may have to keep checking back to see if your question has been answered.

The experts will answer as quickly as they can, but don't expect an immediate reply. Homework help sites receive a great number of questions. They rely on volunteer experts to reply in their free time. You may have to wait several days before you receive your answer.

Portals and study sites

Portal Web sites act as doorways to the rest of the Internet. Education portals usually have a directory of links to other sites on the Internet arranged by school subject. They may also have dictionaries, encyclopedias and other features. Portals are a great place to start when you are looking for ideas for a new project or topic.

Getting started

Education portals are often designed for use by parents and teachers, as well as students. Many also have different information to suit various ages, split into distinct areas of the site. Before you start, make sure you are in the right area.

If the site is not based in your country, check the chart in the homework area of Usborne Quicklinks (go to **www.usborne-quicklinks.com** and enter the keyword **homework**) so that you make sure that the school stage that you consult tallies with the school stage that you are at.

Searching a portal

Portals offer access to a lot of information, so it helps to have a clear idea of what you're looking for before you start. Most of them have a list of categories (usually school subjects) on their home page, so check this first to see if one matches the subject you want. Alternatively, look for a "Site index", which will provide a long list of everything on the site, arranged in alphabetical order.

If you're still not sure where to look, try entering your topic into the site's search field. A successful search will return a list of Web sites for you to try. Portals which review the sites they list will generally mention first the ones they rate most highly.

Many education portals contain directories, which you can use to research different aspects of a subject – right from its broadest categories down to in-depth, specialist information.

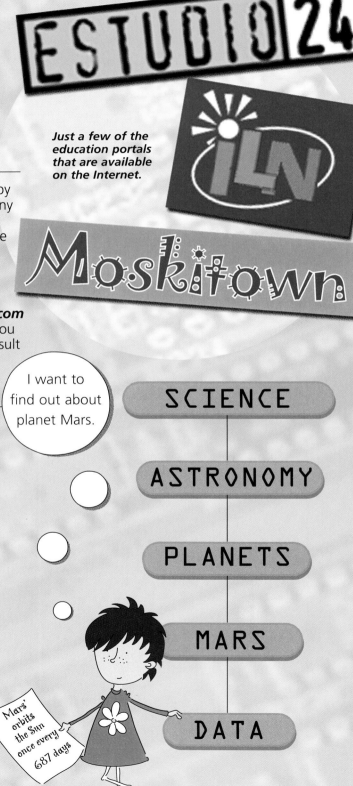

Just a few of the education portals that are available on the Internet.

I want to find out about planet Mars.

SCIENCE

ASTRONOMY

PLANETS

MARS

DATA

Mars' orbits the Sun once every 687 days

Examinations

If you need to study for tests or exams, there are specialist Web sites to help you. Those that are written in America are called "review" sites, while ones that originate in the UK, and many other English-speaking places, tend to be called "revision" sites. Look out for both.

What's on these sites?

Most review, or revision, sites offer multiple-choice tests and lessons based on topics that you will probably have come across in school. Other sites have games and puzzles. Sites are usually geared to a particular country's school system, so you may find, say, a British site to be less useful if you study in the USA, and vice versa.

Using a site

First, pick the level you need to revise at. Next, choose a subject. You can either search through the site's own categories or enter a topic into its search engine. Some sites have links to information held on other Web sites.

Many of these sites organize their information into lessons that summarize a topic's most important aspects. Many generate multiple-choice questions at the end of each lesson for you to try. Some let you save your results, so you can keep tabs on how you improve.

Internet links

For links to all these sites, go to **www.usborne-quicklinks.com** and type the keyword **homework**.

BBC Online Resources for students at school and home. (UK)

Big Chalk Aims to be the single education destination trusted by teachers, used by students, and relied on by parents. (USA)

Education.com This resource has links to other sites, including four sections of education.com in France, Germany, the UK and the USA, and the Moskitown Web site too.

Interactive Learning Network Provides access to useful education sites, plus lessons in sciences. (USA)

Learn.co.uk An educational portal and revision site with subject areas organized into different levels. (UK)

Helping you to help yourself

Many review, or revision, sites also offer a more personalized study service. Some, for instance, ask you questions which help you to identify your strongest and weakest study skills, and give advice on how to deal with them. Others allow you to create your own personal study plan or exam timetable, which you can use whenever you log into the site. You have to register for this kind of service, but it's usually free.

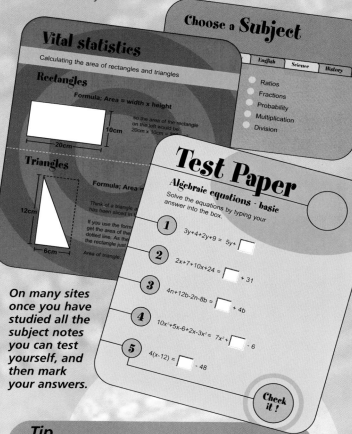

On many sites once you have studied all the subject notes you can test yourself, and then mark your answers.

Tip

Many review, or revision, sites offer a wide range of subjects, but don't try to do too many at once. Concentrating on one or two subjects a day is a good idea, so that you don't end up feeling confused or overloaded with too much information.

Copying and pasting text

It is easy to copy text from a Web page, and paste (insert) it into another document. This enables you to put all your useful research information into one document, which you can refer to later when you write up your homework. Don't be tempted simply to cut and paste other people's writing and pretend it's all your own work... that's cheating, and it will get you into trouble.

Copy

① Display the Web page containing the information that you want to use. Then, using your mouse, place the cursor where you want to start copying. Press the left-hand button on your mouse and hold it down.

② Keeping the left-hand mouse button pressed down, drag the cursor down to the point where you want to stop copying. This highlights and selects the text you want to copy.

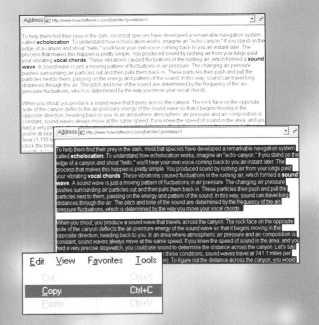

③ Now open your browser's **Edit** menu and click on **Copy**.

Paste

① Open your word processing program, then open the document into which you want to insert your copied text. (For details on opening a basic word processing package, see page 40.)

② Position the cursor where you want the text to appear. Then open the word processing program's **Edit** menu and click on **Paste**.

③ The text you copied from the Web page will appear in your document.

Extracts

You can back up what you say in your homework with a few short extracts of text taken directly from Web sites (or any other reputable source, for that matter). This can add authority to a good piece of work. If you do use an extract, make it clear that the words are not your own by including details of where it came from.

You can separate the extract from your own text by *putting it in italics*...

or "enclosing it in quotation marks".

If it is a long passage, put your quote in a separate paragraph...

or use a combination of any of the above.

Legal stuff

Most companies don't mind if you use their text in a personal project, as long as you include details of where you obtained the information.

However, most of them forbid you to include the information in a document which will be distributed publicly, such as in a school newspaper, without their permission. They will also object if you use their information to earn money.

To find a Web site's rules about the use of its material, scroll down to the bottom of its home page. Most likely, there will be a link to details of its terms of use. Look for hyperlinked phrases such as "Terms of use", "Terms and Conditions", "Copyright details", or simply "Copyright".

Add your own links

It's possible to add your own hyperlinks to your work, if you are using one of the more sophisticated word processing packages, such as Microsoft® Word. People who read your homework on an Internet-connected computer can then jump swiftly to the Web page that you refer to.

To cut and paste an address from a Web page, start by displaying the page that you want. Then make a single click, using your mouse, on the address itself, which is displayed at the top of the Web page. The address will now become highlighted, as in the example below.

Address | http://www.usborne-quicklinks.com/

Next, click on the word **Edit**, and then select **Copy**.

Edit	View	Favorites	Tools
Cut			Ctrl+X
Copy			Ctrl+C
Paste			Ctrl+V

Display the document that you would like to paste into, and position the cursor where you want the address to appear.

Now click on **Edit**, and then **Paste**. If your document is capable of hyperlinking, the address will turn red, or blue, or some other shade. It will also become underlined. This confirms that a hyperlink has been created.

http://www.usborne-quicklinks.com

Hyperlinks also work if you put your document into an e-mail package, such as Microsoft® Outlook Express. Even if you use less sophisticated word processing software, such as Microsoft WordPad (which comes with every copy of Microsoft Windows®) you can add the Web address, so that the reader can cut and paste the exact details into their browser, if they wish to look at the page.

Using pictures

It is easy to copy any picture that you see on the Internet, and put it into your homework in seconds. But if you do this, you need to avoid legal problems, by checking Web sites' copyright details before you copy anything from them (see "Legal stuff", page 35). The instructions shown here refer to Microsoft® Internet Explorer.

How to copy a picture

1. Display the Web page that contains the picture that you want to use. Position your mouse pointer over the picture, then click on the right-hand mouse button.

2. A menu will appear. Click **Copy**.

Pasting a picture

1. Open the document that you want to place the image into. Position the mouse pointer where you want the picture to appear and click once to make the cursor appear in the correct place.

2. Click on the **Edit** menu at the top of the document. Then click on **Paste**. The picture will appear in the document.

Clipart Web sites

Clipart is the name for pictures designed for use in personal documents or on personal Web pages. It is generally free of charge, and you don't have to ask permission from the artist or owner unless you are using the pictures for a commercial purpose.

There are so many clipart Web sites that searching for an image to use in a homework project can be really time consuming. Keep your searching as focused as possible. For example, if you want clipart of a tiger, enter the words *tiger clipart* into a search engine.

***These images are taken from two clipart Web sites:* Free Clipart Island *and* Discovery School.**

Microsoft Paint

Once you have downloaded pictures, it is possible to make basic changes to them, using Microsoft® Paint.

To open Paint, click on your **Start** button, at the bottom left-hand corner of your screen. A menu pops up. Point to **Programs**, and then **Accessories**. Near the bottom of the next menu you'll see **Paint**. Click on that to launch Microsoft Paint.

To open a picture file in Paint click on **File**, choose **Open** and then select the image that you wish to view.

In Paint, you can remove backgrounds, using the eraser tool.

You can alter a picture's borders, using the cropping tool.

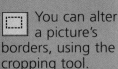

You can rotate the picture by clicking on **Image**, then **Flip/Rotate**.

All these images were downloaded from the Web.

Picture resources

There are lots of picture Web sites, which provide wonderful images, including photographs of wildlife, places, famous people and events.

Keep a record

When you copy a picture from a Web site, note where you got it from, and, if possible, the name of the person who made the image. As a courtesy, put these details next to the picture in your homework. It will also show your teacher that you have taken care when finding the image that you have used.

Important legal tip

If you wish to include downloaded pictures in documents that will be sold, get written permission from the pictures' owners first. It's illegal not to. This applies even if you change the downloaded pictures radically using picture-editing software.

Internet links

For links to all these sites, go to **www.usborne-quicklinks.com** and type the keyword **homework**.

FreeStockPhotos A selection of royalty free and copyright free photographs.

Classroom Clipart Contains loads of images, organized into themes for easy searching.

NASA Image eXchange A searchable archive of NASA's famous space photographs.

FreeFoto Contains a wide range of photographs. Includes images of nature, different countries, industry and transport.

Pics4Learning A photo library put together especially for students. Has links to other free images on the Web.

The Amazing Picture Machine A searchable collection of images specially selected to help students and schools.

Compiling information

With clearly focused Web searching, you should be able to find your homework information quickly. Follow the tips on these two pages to maximize your effectiveness.

Limit your time online

Keep in mind that once you have found information on the Web, you will still have to spend time actually doing your homework. Spending ages online will just result in homework taking longer to do. So be ruthless – search as quickly as you can.

The first way to do this is to set yourself an amount of time online, say 30 minutes. (If you are not on a free Internet service, you will be paying for the cost of using the Web anyway, so cutting down on your online time will save you money.)

Use trusted sites

Start by consulting famous encyclopedias, where you are likely to get a good grounding in the key facts, then follow the links that they give, or go to education Web sites and portals to find extra information.

As you get more used to the Internet, you will find that there are a number of sites that you trust. You'll find that you use this small group of sites again and again.

However, try not to become reliant on information from one source, or a narrow selection of sites. Other sites will have extra information that you can use, to give your homework an added dimension.

Tip

Once you've found the information that you seek on a Web site, move on as fast as you can. Don't be tempted to linger on any site. It's a waste of time – you'll have less time to spend actually doing your homework.

Words first... pictures later

If you find pictures while you are searching for information and you think they might be useful in your homework, there's no harm in saving them as you go along.

Don't fall into the trap of just looking at the images on Web sites, though. Unless you are specifically looking for certain pictures, it's best to find your information before you go looking for specific images. For details on copying and pasting pictures, go back to page 36.

Pictures and captioned diagrams can convey useful information, as well as brightening up your work.

Store the best stuff

If you find some information that you think might be useful, you could copy and paste it into a word processing document. This way, you can build up a list of useful articles, quotations and passages in one document. These sources will be useful to you when you come to write up your homework.

To do this, follow these steps:

1 Find, copy, and paste the text into a word processing document (see page 34).

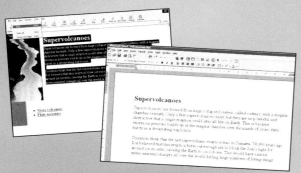

2 After you've pasted the text, copy and paste the Web address from the **Address** box at the top of the browser. Paste the address close to the text you have just copied. It will help you to keep tabs on your sources, in case you need to go back to the Web site later.

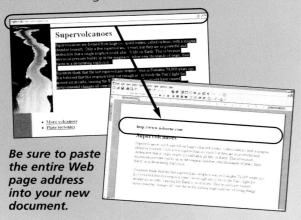

Be sure to paste the entire Web page address into your new document.

Tip

Keeping a record of which piece of information comes from which Web site provides you with a ready-made list of credits. Use it to compile a bibliography – a record of the sources of information that you have used in your homework.

History and Favorites

Use the **History** and **Favorites** buttons to make use of information on sites you have visited previously. For details on how to do this, take a look back at pages 12-13.

Beware hyperlinks

When you paste text from a Web page into a basic word processing document, such as WordPad, anything that was hyperlinked in the original document, such as:

ct all volcanoes could

may change, becoming a piece of HTML (see page 8). The basic text will still be readable, but you may have to go through and edit out the strange-looking computer instructions, such as:

volcanoes <../glossary/glossary.html>

If you have more sophisticated word processing software, such as Microsoft® Word, the hyperlink will be retained, as shown below.

fact all volcanoes could

Word processing basics

After you've found the information that you need from the Internet, you'll be using your computer again – this time to write your homework, correct it and make it look attractive. To do this, use word processing software. If you're new to word processing, read these pages. If you've used it before you can move on and read the four pages starting from page 42.

Word processing software

All modern personal computers have word processing software. For example, computers that use Microsoft® Windows® have software called WordPad. It's fairly basic, so it's easy to use. Also, the way it works is similar to many other types of word processing software. If you start using something else, you'll find the differences are not too startling.

WordPad

To open WordPad, click on the **Start** button at the bottom left-hand corner of your screen.

Point your mouse pointer at **Programs**, then **Accessories**. A drop-down menu will appear. At the bottom of this menu, you'll see an icon and the name **WordPad**. Click on it once and the program will launch.

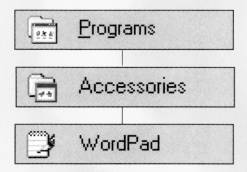

WordPad opens quickly. At the top, you'll see tools and drop-down commands displayed, just as you do with your Web browser. Underneath is a big blank area, where your words and pictures will go.

Type in your work carefully. As you type, WordPad will line up the words automatically on the left of the page.

Making changes

Using word processing packages, it's easy to delete or move words around. To do this, you need to start by selecting the text you want to alter.

(1) Position your mouse pointer to the left of the words you want to select and press down on your left-hand mouse button.

> Volcanoes poured out red-hot liquid

(2) Keep the button pressed down, and drag your mouse across the words, so that they become highlighted. Release your mouse button when your chosen words are highlighted.

> Volcanoes poured out red-hot liquid

Deleting text

To delete a block of text:

(1) Click on the highlighted text with the right-hand mouse button. A menu of choices will appear.

Cut
Copy
Paste

Font...
Bullet Style
Paragraph...

Object Properties
Object

(2) Click on **Cut**. The text will disappear.

Cut

Moving text

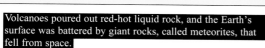

1 Highlight the text that you want to move.

> Volcanoes poured out red-hot liquid rock, and the Earth's surface was battered by giant rocks, called meteorites, that fell from space.
>
> For millions of years after the Earth was formed, nothing could live there. There was no water, no breathable air, and no protection from the harmful rays of the Sun.

2 Then click with your right hand mouse button so that a menu appears. Choose **Cut** and the text will vanish.

> Cut
> Copy
> Paste
>
> Font...
> Bullet Style
> Paragraph...
>
> Object Properties
> Object

3 Now position the cursor in the new place that you want your text to appear.

> For millions of years after the Earth was formed, nothing could live there. There was no water, no breathable air, and no protection from the harmful rays of the Sun.
>
> |

4 Click with your right hand mouse button, so that the menu of choices reappears. Click on **Paste**. The text will now appear in its new position.

> Paste

> For millions of years after the Earth was formed, nothing could live there. There was no water, no breathable air, and no protection from the harmful rays of the Sun.
>
> Volcanoes poured out red-hot liquid rock, and the Earth's surface was battered by giant rocks, called meteorites, that fell from space.

Arranging text

Word processing software enables you to position text in different ways on the page.

1 To put words in the middle of the line, highlight the words, then click on this button.

2 To miss a line, press the Return key on your keyboard twice.

3 To put words on the left of the page, highlight the words, then click on this button.

4 To put words on the right of the page, highlight the words, then click on this button.

These buttons were used to arrange the text shown below.

> *The Earth* —————— **1**
>
> *Part 1 - A lifeless planet* —————— **2**
>
> *For millions of years after the Earth was formed, nothing could live there. There was no water, no breathable air, and no protection from the harmful rays of the Sun.*
>
> *Volcanoes poured out red-hot liquid rock, and the Earth's surface was battered by giant rocks, called meteorites, which fell from space.* —————— **3**
>
> *By Molly Brown* —————— **4**

For more information about changing the appearance of your homework documents, see pages 44-45.

Software purchasing

You can buy word processing software. It contains features that enable you to make more sophisticated document layouts. Also, it enables you to do automatic hyperlinking (see page 35), and checks your spelling and grammar, too.

Editing

The process of editing your work begins when you start choosing what information to include in your homework. It goes on as you choose the words that you want to write, and finishes as you check, amend and correct the text that you have written. Use the tips on these pages to help you become a top editor.

Plan it first

Before you start researching, make a rough plan of what you will say. List the main points that you want to include in your homework. This will help focus your research.

Rough plan - Sharks

How many types?   Where do they live?

All killers? All dangerous?   What are their teeth like?

Does anything eat them?

Sizes?   How long do they live?   Are they whales?

— Biggest?   Do they sleep?   Warm blooded?

— Smallest?   Birth? - varies depending   Other related fish?
on type.

Researching

Look at things that you might have been taught in class, check out encyclopedia articles, text books — whatever you think will be useful. Don't forget to use the Web, too.

Keep researching your subject until you have found all the information that you need. If you realize that there are things that you want to say, but you haven't found the information yet, go back to the Web and find it at this stage.

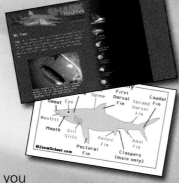

Here's some research on sharks, found on the Web.

When you have finished researching, you are ready to make a detailed plan.

Detailed planning

Sharks Project Plan

— INTRO — 368 types, smallest 15cm (lantern shark), largest 18 metres (whale shark) —www.enchantedlearning.com

— Birth of sharks varies — www.geocities.com/SouthBeach/Marina/4077/Shark.txt

— Eating habits — from plankton to seals and sea lions — www.seaworld.org/infobooks/Sharks&Rays/diet.html

— Dangerous sharks — Great white, bull, nurse, tiger — www.sharkfriends.com

— Harmless sharks — Basking, whale shark, Greenland — www.seaworld.com

— Statistics on shark attacks on humans — www.enchantedlearning.com

A detailed plan should include the major points that you wish to make. Jot down where you will get your information from for each point – this will make it easier for you to find and use the information that you have researched.

The tightly structured approach to planning will ensure that you stay in control of what you are writing. It's a technique that professional writers use.

Don't forget to download pictures that you want to use.

Remember this

When you are researching, never just base your homework on just one source. If you do, you'll end up duplicating information from the only piece you use. Using information from multiple sources gives you a better range of material to choose from. A selection of sources will also enable you to cross-check your details, so that you are more likely to use information that is correct.

Say it your way

When you are writing, put down what you want to say in your own words. Include useful information from Web sites, or anywhere else, by rewriting it in your own style. When you have finished writing, take a break.

After your break, come back and edit your document. Start by reading it through, checking it for spelling errors and badly written sentences. Be ruthless at this stage. If anything doesn't sound right, re-do it so that you are happy with what you are saying. Ignore things now and you will become blind to the mistakes you have made. You'll kick yourself when they are pointed out by your teacher.

It's worth the effort

By rewriting information in your own words, you are showing that you have made the effort to take in information, understand it, and express it your own way. Teachers want you to prove that you can do this – it's what learning is all about. That's why they want to read something that you have written yourself.

Watch out – plagiarism (copying someone else's stuff) will land you in deep water.

Don't cheat

Whatever you do, don't try to get away with passing off text from a Web site, or any other source, as your own. For a start, you won't be learning anything by doing it, so it won't do you any good. Secondly, because it's a form of cheating, all teachers, from schools right up to universities, take a dim view of it. Thirdly, most teachers are good at spotting this type of thing – so chances are you'll get caught.

The occasional quote

There may be pieces of information that you find on the Web that you really want to paste into your document, as direct quotes. Add them as you are writing, and always include the details of where you found them.

"There is no shark that naturally feeds on man..."
(www.geocities.com/South Beach/Palms/8718/myths.html)

You won't get a better grade for adding direct quotes unless they are good, so do it with care. If you choose well, this technique can add authority to well-researched work. Also, use just a few concise quotes – they are more effective than frequent long passages.

Internet links

For links to all these sites, go to **www.usborne-quicklinks.com** and type the keyword **homework**.

The Arrow A fun-to-read site that shows you how to plan and write assignments.

Encarta Research Organizer A download that will help you to research and organize your work.

The Online English Grammar A good Web site for improving your grasp of English.

ILN Research Papers Suggestions and resources for those who are stuck for a project research topic.

Plagiarism Q&A Find out all about plagiarism and why you should avoid it.

Fact Monster Homework Center An in-depth resource on how to write essays, reports, biographies and bibliographies.

Looking good

To top off a well-researched, well-written piece of homework, you have to make sure that it is well presented, too. Choosing a clear, readable type style, or font, and skilfully arranging pictures are part of this process. Get it wrong and your document will look like a dog's dinner. Get it right, and it will look like a million dollars.

Add your images

When you are happy with your text you can begin to add your images. First, choose where you would like them to go. Then, to insert a picture, take a look back at page 36.

Repositioning a picture

Once you have added a picture, you can move it around by "dragging and dropping" it. To do this, place your mouse pointer over the picture, then press down the left mouse button. Drag your mouse pointer to a new position, then release the button. The picture will move.

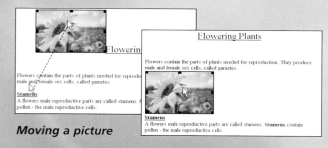

Moving a picture

You can also position a picture in the middle, left or right of the page. Select the picture by clicking on it, then click on one of the position buttons on the format bar.

The position buttons

Resizing a picture

To make a picture bigger or smaller in WordPad, click on the picture. A frame with eight handles will appear. When you hold your mouse over a handle, it turns into a pointing hand. Click on a pointing hand, and it becomes a resizing arrow.

— **Handle**

Resizing arrow

You can resize the picture by clicking on a handle and dragging it.

Give your picture a caption

Picture captions are quick explanations of a picture which go near the image itself. Use type that is smaller than your document's main text. Keep captions brief and relevant to the picture.

Avoid the things shown in the example on the right, including:
- long, rambling sentences
- bad grammar and spelling
- irrelevant information.

A decent caption

Sunflowers can reach heights of 1.8m (6ft).

A dreadful caption

Flowers contain petels, stamens, carpels etc etc etc this is so they can reporduce. Some smell, but not all, this is to attract insetcs that they need to reproduce like bees which like to drink nectar.

Font selection

WordPad automatically uses a font called Times New Roman. You can tell which font and size is used by looking near the top of the screen. Size is measured in units called points (pt).

This is part of WordPad's format bar.

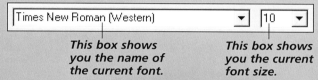

This box shows you the name of the current font.

This box shows you the current font size.

Changing fonts

(1) Select the text that you want to change. Then, on the format bar, click on the arrow in the font drop-down list box. An alphabetical list of names of fonts will appear. Click on one, such as Helvetica.

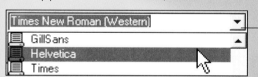

Click here to display a list of fonts

(2) To change the size of the letters in a word, first select them. On the format bar, click on the arrow in the letter size drop-down list box. Choose another size from the list. The best sizes for long sections of text are 10 and 12. Use bigger sizes, such as sizes 18 or 24, for headings.

Here is a selection of font sizes, and styles.

This is 10pt Helvetica.

This is 12pt Times New Roman.

This is 18pt Amerigo.

This is 24pt Arial.

Emphasizing words

To make words italic, select them, then click on this button on the format bar.

 make your words italic

To make words bold, select them, then click on this button on the format bar.

 make your words bold

To underline words, select them, then click on this button on the format bar.

 <u>underline your words</u>

Make it simple

In a homework project, try not to use more than two different fonts. Any more than this and the document will start to look messy, making it no fun to read.

Keep it simple

For your main text, choose a font that is relatively plain and easy to read – nothing too swirly or decorative. Your teacher will soon tire of a font that is not easy on the eye, no matter how lovely you think it is.

Get organized

Saving your work is important – if you don't you'll have wasted all the effort that you put into doing your homework in the first place. It's best to save it in an orderly way, so that you'll be able to find it again quickly when you need it. To keep your files all neat and tidy, get into the habit of keeping them in folders.

A folder for homework

Start by creating a particular place on your computer where you can store all your homework. To do this, follow these instructions.

(1) Display the basic Windows® desktop. (This is the screen that appears when your machine has just completed its start-up procedure.) Little icons appear on the desktop, usually down the left-hand side. One of these is called **My Computer**.

This is the "My Computer" icon.

(2) Click on **My Computer**, and a window will spring open, showing the various disk drives that are on your computer, plus several other folders. A typical example is shown on the right.

(3) The icon marked **(C:)** is your hard disk. This is a magnetic disk that stores all your computer's information, including all the programs that have been loaded onto it. Double-click on the icon, and the folders that contain the contents of your hard drive will be displayed.

(4) To make a new folder, click with the right hand mouse button, and a box containing a selection of choices will appear. Point the mouse cursor at **New**, then click on **Folder**.

(5) A new folder will appear, which is simply called **New Folder**. Now type the word "Homework" and the folder's name will immediately change to **Homework**.

Using the Homework folder

To save a piece of work into the Homework folder, start with an open file. (It's best to try this on an empty file, one that you've simply opened and not worked in, just in case you make a mistake.)

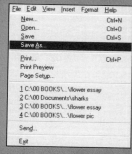

(1) With the file open, click on **File** on the menu bar. A menu will appear.

(2) Click on **Save As**. A box called a dialog box will appear. You use dialog boxes to give information to your computer.

(3) Click on the arrow in the drop-down list box called **Save in** to open a list of parts of your computer.

(4) Click on the icon marked **(C:)**, the hard disk. Icons for the folders in the hard disk will appear in the main part of the dialog box.

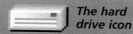

The hard drive icon

(5) Double-click on the icon for your Homework folder.

(6) In the box called **File name**, type a descriptive name for your file, so you can remember which piece of homework it contains. Keep it short. Your computer won't let you use the following symbols in your filename: / \ * < > ? " :

(7) Click on the **Save** button.

Subfolders

Folders within folders are called subfolders. After a while you may find that your homework folder is beginning to get a little crowded and messy. To make things more ordered, create subfolders within the homework folder. You could create folders for different subjects.

To create a subfolder:

(1) Open the homework folder by double-clicking on its icon.

Homework

(2) Click with the right-hand mouse button, and a box containing a selection of choices will appear. Point the mouse cursor at **New**, then click on **Folder**.

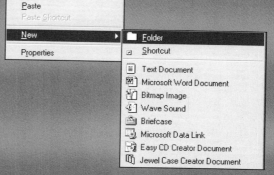

(3) A new folder will appear, called **New Folder**. Now type the name that you want to give to this folder, say "Geography". The folder's name will immediately change to Geography.

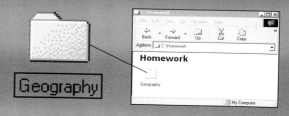

Geography

Hard copy

Hard copy is a name given to computer-generated work that has been printed out on paper. Once you've finished your homework you will probably want to make a hard copy of it, ready to be presented. These pages will show you how. The details refer to programs including Microsoft® WordPad, Word and Paint.

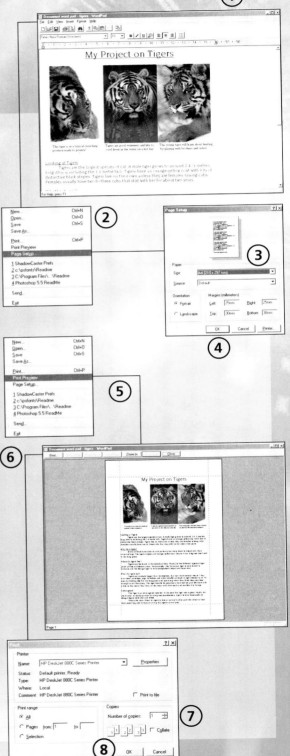

Printing out

1. Open the document that you want to print.

2. Click on **File** menu, then choose **Page Setup**. A Page Setup dialog box will appear.

3. Choose the same paper size as the paper in your printer. If you want, change the printing orientation and the sizes of the margins. This will affect the way the page looks.

4. When you think that the page is set up to your needs, click **OK**.

5. Now click on **Print Preview** in the **File** menu. The Print Preview window will appear. This shows you exactly how your work will appear on paper. If you want to make changes, you need to close the Print Preview window before you can alter your document or picture. Open the Print Preview window again to check any changes you make.

6. In the Print Preview window, click on the **Print...** button. A Print dialog box will appear. This contains information about the name of the printer you are using, and the size and orientation of the paper. (You may have to click on a button called **Properties** or **Options** to see all the information in the dialog box.)

7. You can change the information that tells the computer which pages and how many copies you want.

8. Click **OK** to finish. Soon printing will begin.

Orientation

Orientation refers to the way that a page looks: tall or wide. Tall-looking pages are called portrait – it's the standard way that pictures of people are presented. Wide-looking pages are called landscape. This is because images of the land are usually wide, so that as much of the scene as possible is shown. To set orientation, choose **Page Setup**, then make your choice in the **Orientation** box.

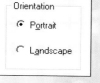

Landscape shape

Portrait shape

Margins

Margin

A margin is a blank area between the edge of your work and the edge of the paper. Each page you print will have four margins: left, right, top and bottom. The computer will automatically choose a width for each margin, but you can change these.

To change your margins, click on the **File** menu, then choose **Page Setup**. The Page Setup box will appear, and within it the **Margins** box as shown above. For best results with typed documents, make sure that your margins are at least 15mm ($\frac{1}{2}$in).

Quick print

Printers usually have settings that allow you to print things out at various qualities. Printing things out in rough, or low, quality has advantages, particularly if you want to make a hard copy of a document that you haven't completed. For a start, it means that you get your printout quickly. Secondly, it means that you don't use up your printer's ink, which is expensive to buy.

Tip

When you take a break from writing, make a rough print of the work you have just done. When you come back to it, read through the printout, jotting down any comments and corrections that occur to you as you read through. You'll find it much easier to spot errors on paper than on the computer screen.

After you have finished your read through, go back to your computer to make the necessary changes to your document.

Save the trees

If you are going to print out a rough copy of your work, you could print it out on the back of sheets of paper that you've used and no longer want. That way you won't use up so much paper, which will ultimately mean that you won't have such a big paper bill... and you'll save trees, too.

Moving your work

Now that you've done your homework project, it's time to take it into school. You could print it out at home, if you like, but there are alternatives. You could download it onto a disk and carry it, or send it electronically as an e-mail attachment. If you're new to e-mail, read about the basics first. Over the page, you'll find the low-down on putting work onto disks.

Opening an e-mail program

There are many different e-mail programs available, but the most widely used is Microsoft® Outlook Express. To open Outlook Express click on your **Start** button and from the menu select **Programs** then **Outlook Express.**

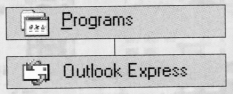

Alternatively, if you have the Outlook Express icon displayed on your desktop, click on that. Outlook Express will open immediately.

This is the Outlook Express icon which may appear on your desktop.

E-mail addresses

Here's a typical e-mail address:

joeschmo@slugpost.com

This is the name that the person has decided to use when sending and receiving e-mails.

@ stands for "at".

slugpost.com is the domain name. For home computer users, this is normally the name of your ISP.

Send and receive

① Click on the **New Mail** button on the toolbar. A window entitled **New Message** will open.

New mail

② Don't forget – you'll need to put the e-mail address of the person you're writing to in the panel to the right of **To:**. Also, write a title for your message in the panel to the right of **Subject**.

③ Click in the main panel and type your message.

④ To finish, click the **Send** button. Your message will be sent as soon as you are next online.

Send

⑤ Click on **Send and Receive**. Your computer connects to the Internet and sends messages from the Outbox. If there are new messages for you, your computer will collects them.

Send and receive

Tip

If you are charged for your time online, set Outlook Express to disconnect as soon as your e-mail has downloaded. To do this, click on **Tools**, then **Options**, then **Connection**, then choose **Hang up after sending and receiving**.

E-mail attachment

To send your assignment as an attachment to an e-mail message, first open Outlook Express. Click on the **New Mail** button to create a new e-mail, put the address of the recipient in the **Address** panel, and the subject in the Subject panel. Then type a message, if you want. Then:

(1) Click on the **Attach** symbol at the top of the **New Message** box.

Attach

(2) A window called **Insert Attachment** will open. Find and choose the file that you want to attach to your message.

(3) Click on the **Attach** button.

(4) The name of the file that you have attached, along with an icon, showing what type of file it is, will appear in a new panel at the top of the message.

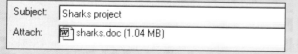

(5) Press the **Send** button to send your message with added attachments.

Send

Check your size

Before you send an attachment, it's best to check that the file you want to send is not so big that it will gum up your connection for ages while it is squeezed down the phone lines. Take a look at page 54 to see a rule of thumb for assessing what is, and what is not an acceptable size, depending on what type of Internet connection you have.

Zip it up

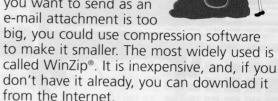

If you find that the file you want to send as an e-mail attachment is too big, you could use compression software to make it smaller. The most widely used is called WinZip®. It is inexpensive, and, if you don't have it already, you can download it from the Internet,

Using WinZip

(1) Open WinZip. Then click on the **New** icon to create a folder, which will hold the file, or files, that you are about to compress. Give the folder a name.

New

(2) As soon as you've named the folder, a window entitled **Add** pops up. Choose the file that you want to compress, then select the level of compression that you would like, such as **Maximum (slowest)**. Then click **Add**.

(3) As the file compresses, a little icon at the bottom-right of WinZip turns from green to red. When it has finished, the icon turns green again.

 The red icon indicates that the file is being compressed.

 The green icon indicates that the compressed file is ready.

The compressed file's name is now added to the folder.

As well as details of the file, WinZip will show you the original size, compression ratio, and the compressed size of the file. If the compression ratio is very large, then the file will send much more quickly than it would if you tried to send it uncompressed.

Downloading to disks

If you want to move a homework project, you might prefer to download it onto a disk, rather than send it as an e-mail attachment, or print it out. The type of disk that you use will depend on two things: first, what disk drives you have on your computer; second, the size of file that you wish to download.

Portable disks

Before you put your homework onto a disk, check that the disk is big enough to hold it. (You can find out the size of a document by highlighting its icon, clicking with the right-hand mouse button, and choosing **Properties**.) Also, be sure that the computer you use at school has a similar disk drive, so that it can download the information at the other end.

Floppy disk

This is the most commonly available, and low-priced disk. It's small, light, and easy to use. All modern computers have floppy disk drives. They have one drawback though: they only hold 1.44Mb of information. Your homework may be too big to fit on the disk.

You may have to compress your homework (see page 51) to get it onto a floppy disk.

Iomega Zip disk

Iomega® Zip® disks look like chunky floppy disks. They hold either 100Mb or 250Mb of information, depending on which version you buy. You need to have a special Zip disk drive to make them work.

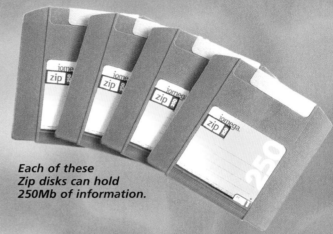

Each of these Zip disks can hold 250Mb of information.

CD-R

CD-R is a CD that you can write onto (the "R" stands for recordable). To do this you need to have a special CD writer, and they are not cheap. CD-Rs hold 650Mb of information and they can be read using just about any CD drive. CD writer software works in various ways, so follow the instructions on your own writer.

CD-Rs look just like regular CDs.

Filling a floppy

(1) Start by putting a floppy disk into the floppy disk drive in your computer.

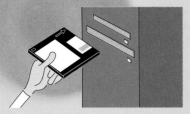

(2) Find and open the folder containing your homework.

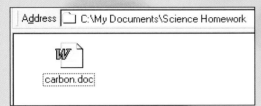

(3) Click on the My Computer icon on your desktop. Now click on the icon that is named **3½ Floppy**. The contents of the floppy disk that you just put into the drive will now be displayed.

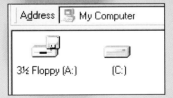

(4) Arrange the folder containing your homework and the folder showing the contents of the floppy disk, side-by-side.

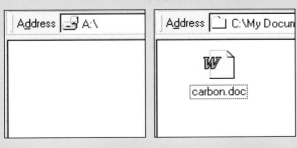

(5) Now, point your mouse pointer at the icon for the homework project that you'd like to put on to the floppy. Click and hold down on the icon, using your left-hand mouse button.

(6) Continuing to hold down with your left-hand mouse button, drag your mouse pointer across to the floppy drive's window. The folder will be dragged across with it.

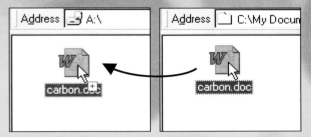

(7) Let go of the button, and the folder will be copied onto the floppy disk.

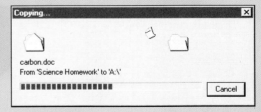

Follow these instructions for putting work onto Zip disks – it's the same process.

Tip

Always make sure that you give a printed version of your homework to your teacher. The last thing they want to have to do is print out their students' homework before they sit down and mark it all.

Getting connected

Around the world, most people who use the Internet still gain access using an ordinary telephone line and a device called a modem. This is the cheapest option... but it's also the slowest. The details on these pages show you some possible alternatives.

Connection speeds

Type of connection	What's the benefit?	What's the catch?
Modem and phone line Data is transferred at a rate of around 40Kbps (often written 40K). At best, a modem can download or send a 1MB file in about 2.5 minutes.	It's inexpensive. It's easy to set up, too.	It's slow. You have to wait while the modem connects to the Internet, which gets boring... Also, it ties up your phone line, so nobody can speak to you on the phone while you're online.
ISDN Has a connection speed of up to 128Kbps. Can send or download a 1Mb file in around a minute. Uses regular telephone lines, in pairs, or new digital telephone lines.	Up to three times as fast as a regular modem-phone line combination.	Costs more to set up than a regular modem-phone line combination. Monthly line rental charges can be higher, too.
xDSL There are various versions of this – ADSL and SDSL are the most often used, at present. Uses sophisticated digital technology to pack lots of data onto regular phone cables. With either, download speeds are higher than ISDN.	Enables quick Web surfing – great when you're researching your homework. Connection to the Internet is always on. This means that you don't have to tell your modem to connect to the Internet, and then twiddle your thumbs while it crunches into life.	In general, this technology costs more to set up than ISDN. ADSL is no quicker than ISDN when it comes to sending things. You have to be close to a telephone switching station to use it: the technology is only feasible from station-to-user, not between stations.
Cable Takes just a few seconds to download or send a 1Mb file. Ideal for homework research and for sending attachments. Uses the same cables that carry cable television signals.	It's very quick, both for sending and receiving files. The connection to the Internet is always on... so you don't waste time waiting for connections to start up.	You have to have a cable television connection to your house, and this service may not be available where you live. Is about as expensive as an ISDN connection to set up.

Browser software

Internet browsing software is included with all new personal computers. The vast majority use Microsoft® Internet Explorer, but other browsers, such as Netscape® Communicator, are as good.

There are browsers that are designed specifically for children. Examples include ChiBrow® and SurfMonkey®, which you can download. If you use these, you will be steered towards child-friendly sites, and protected from any potentially offensive material.

Services

The information that you send and receive is processed by a company that gives you quick and easy access to the Internet. You can choose which company gives you these services. There are two ways that you can access the Internet with the minimum of fuss.

Internet service providers (**ISPs**) These are companies that store and sort your requests for information (see how they connect to the Internet on pages 5-6). They also provide you with access to e-mail and technical support. ISPs will give you space on their servers so you can publish your own Web site on the Internet.

Online services These work like ISPs, but they offer extra services, such as news, entertainment information, online shopping, all within a click or two of the home page. They also block Web sites that they deem unsuitable.

Internet links

For links to all these sites, go to *www.usborne-quicklinks.com* and type the keyword **homework**.

Internet 101 Contains overviews of ISPs and browsers, with many useful links.

Welcome to the Web A Web site that will help you to learn all about the Internet.

Glossary of Internet Terms A mega-sized list of all the techy Internet terms that you're ever likely to meet – and more.

Choosing a service

Before deciding which ISP or online service to use, bear in mind the following:

- Why pay for the service? Many ISPs are free. If there is a charge, make sure that you'll be getting more for your money than you would from a free-to-use provider.

- What charges will you run up while you are online? For a basic modem-phone line connection, ISPs and online services generally guarantee that your costs will be no more than that of a local call. Some even offer free call costs, for a small monthly fee.

- Does the ISP have technical support advisors whom you can call for help? How much does the service cost? Is it free? How long will you have to wait to speak to someone?

- Ask people you know who use the Internet to give you their impressions of the service providers that they use. Follow the recommendations of those you trust.

- Can the ISP or online service be accessed using high-speed links, such as ISDN and ADSL? If it does, you'll be able to continue using them if and when you decide to upgrade to a faster link.

- How many e-mail addresses will you get? Nearly all ISPs and online services give you at least one e-mail address. Good providers give more – which means that everyone in your family could have their own private e-mail address.

- Will you want to create your own Web site? If so, you'll need space on your service provider's server. Find out how much they'll provide for you. 5Mb will be enough for a really basic site, but you'll need more if you want to make it more sophisticated.

And don't forget: shop around before you choose a provider.

Avoiding trouble

Much of the information on the Internet is excellent, and will be really useful to you. Some of it, though, is trash that will simply waste your research time... and the worst of it is offensive garbage that will be of absolutely no use to you at all. Chat rooms and message boards can be a waste of time too, and occasionally are spoiled by people whose aim is to upset, offend, or, worse, harm young people. Follow the tips shown here to help you cut out the undesirable.

Try setting your filters

Web browsers, such as Microsoft® Internet Explorer, can be adjusted to cut out certain types of content, which will probably be useless to you. If you wish to adjust your filters:

① Click on **Tools**, Internet **Options**.

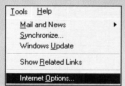

② Across the top of the Internet Options window, click on **Content**.

③ Click the **Enable...** button under the heading Content Adviser

④ Select the category you'd like to adjust. Then move the "slider" to set the limits.

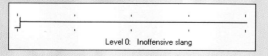

Try safety software

Many Web experts reckon that a good way to stay safe is to use filtering software. Service providers such as AOL and Compuserve have built-in filtering software, so they can cut out the things that they don't want you to see. This doesn't happen if you are using regular ISPs, but you can install filtering programs such as Net Nanny® and CyberPatrol®. These programs check Web sites and hold back those with the type of content that you choose to block.

You'll find this type of program available from most software retailers.

Tip

If a Web page is downloading which you think is going to be unhelpful to you in your research, simply press the **Stop** button. You will immediately end the download, and be able to move on to downloading more useful information straight away.

Stop!

If you come across something on the Web which is illegal, you can report it to an Internet crimefighting organization. See the Internet links box for details.

Chat room safety

If you use a homework chat room, keep in mind that you are there to do research. If the chat strays from what you are trying to research, log off: you're wasting time if you hang around.

Always stay aware of the fact that some adults will gain entry to chat rooms simply because they take a sexual interest in young people, and maybe to try to lure them into a face-to-face meeting.

If things get unpleasant while you're in a chat room and somebody starts writing stuff that is weird or offensive, leave the chat room immediately. Then report the incident to the chat room's monitor or to the site's Webmaster.

Protect personal details

Do not give out personal details when you use chat rooms, message boards or e-mail. This includes your name and address, and your school's name and address. Anyone can read them, which just might result in you getting unwanted attention from somebody you'd rather not meet in the real world.

Meeting up

Do not agree to meet up with somebody whom you meet in a chat room, no matter how nice and genuine they seem. Remember, it's easy to pretend to be almost anyone in a chat room.

Virus vigilance

For some reason, there are people who spend their time creating computer viruses. These are programs that load onto your computer without your knowledge and run against your wishes, in order to damage or destroy your computer.

Many viruses are sent to you as attachments to e-mails, or as part of a program that you load onto your computer. Some are even on disks that have a virus on them. It is important that you don't open attachments or load new software onto your machine unless you are sure that it is from a reputable source.

The only way to be absolutely safe from viruses is to buy anti-virus software from a reputable company, such as Norton® or McAfee®. Make sure that you update the software regularly, since new viruses are being unleashed all the time.

Anti-virus software is available in many languages.

Internet links

For links to all these sites, go to *www.usborne-quicklinks.com* and type the keyword **homework**.

Get Netwise A guide to using the Internet safely, written with families and young people in mind.

Wired Kidz Another Internet guide, for all the family.

Cyberangels Safety tips and hotlines for reporting crime found on the Internet. Based in the USA.

Internet Watch Foundation Another source of safety tips and hotlines for reporting Internet wrongdoing. Based in the UK.

Cyber Patrol® A popular program for filtering Web sites.

Net Nanny® A highly rated filtering program.

Norton AntiVirus™ One of the leading anti-virus programs.

McAfee VirusScan® Another reputable anti-virus program.

Glossary

When computer and Internet-related things are described, specialist words and phrases tend to crop up – making the subject a bit tricky to understand. Use the definitions on these pages to cut the jargon down to size. Words in *italics* are defined elsewhere.in the glossary.

A

address box The box in your Internet *browser* that displays a Web page's *URL*.

ADSL (**Asymetric Digital Subscriber Line**) A type of *DSL* (a high-speed Internet connection) in which the speed at which things are received, the *download* speed, is much greater than the speed at which things are sent, called the upload speed.

applet A small *program* written in the programming language *Java*™. Can be inserted into a *Web page*, to make the page more interactive and entertaining.

application Any *program* which enables your computer to create documents or perform tasks, such as word processing.

attachment A *file* sent with an *e-mail*, which has to be *downloaded* before it can be used.

B

bandwidth A measurement of the amount of *data* that can flow through a link between computers in a fixed amount of time. Usually measured in *bits* per second (bps) or *bytes* per second.

bibliography A list of books or other sources consulted when doing research. (If you consult Internet documents as part of your research, include the name of the *Web site*, its author, and its *URL* in your bibliography.)

bit (**b**inary dig**it**) The smallest unit of *data* used by computers.

boot To start up a computer.

broadband Refers to high-speed *data transfer* between computers.

browser A *program*, such as Microsoft® Internet Explorer, that finds and displays documents stored on the *Web*.

byte A unit of *data*, equivalent to 8 *bits*.

C

cache A computer's temporary memory. Your browser uses it to temporarily remember *Web pages* that you look at, so that you can look at them again later without having to wait as they *download* from the Internet.

CD-Rom (**Compact Disc Read-only memory**) A thin metal-coated plastic plate used to store computer *data*.

chat room A *Web page* where users are able to *post* and read messages instantly.

client A computer that relies on a *server* computer in order to run and store *applications*.

clipart Pictures, usually *copyright*-free, that you can *download* from the Internet to illustrate documents.

clipboard An area of temporary computer memory where a piece of text or an image is stored while the *cut*, *copy* or *paste* commands are in use.

compression The reduction of data contained in a file so that it take up less memory space, enabling it to *upload* and *download* quicker.

connection speed The rate of *data transfer* between one computer and another.

cookie A file sent by a Web *server* to a *browser*. It collects information about what you do while you are viewing the *Web site*.

copy To copy text or an image to a computer's *clipboard*.

copyright The right of ownership of things such as pictures, plays, the words in books and magazines, and so on. Anything that is copyrighted cannot be reproduced without permission from the copyright holder.

crash A sudden failure in a computer system, so that you have to restart (*reboot*) it.

cursor A flashing symbol that appears on your monitor when you are using word processing software. It shows you where you are about to type.

cut To take text or an image from a computer document, and copy it to a computer's *clipboard*.

cyberspace The "world" of the *Internet*, and all that is on it.

D

data Information, especially that processed by a computer.

data transfer The movement of *data* from one computer to another.

directory A type of *search engine* that organizes *Web sites* into categories.

document A type of computer *file*, usually created using word processing software. May contain pictures and graphics, too.

domain name The part of a *URL* that identifies a particular *Web site*, for example, "www.usborne.com".

double-click To click a mouse button twice in rapid succession. Used to open *applications* or *files* in Windows® and on Macintosh® computers.

download 1) To copy a *Web page* or *program* from the *Internet* to your own computer. 2) Something that has been downloaded.

DSL (Digital Subscriber Line) A type of *broadband Internet* connection that uses advanced digital technology to enable large amounts of data to be sent along regular telephone lines very quickly.

E

editing Preparing a document for presentation, involving the processes of selection, checking and correction.

e-mail (electronic mail) A way of sending messages via the *Internet* to other computer users.

encryption Translating information sent across the *Internet* into code, to keep it secure.

extract 1) A section of text quoted in another work. 2) To "unzip" files from a *WinZip®* archive.

F

FAQ (Frequently Asked Questions) In the world of the Internet, this usually refers to part of a *Web site* that contains queries written by visitors to the site. Answers are often provided alongside the questions.

file Anything stored on a computer, such as a *document*, image or *program*.

filter A set of instructions that an Internet browser uses to check whether a Web site is suitable for viewing.

flame An overly harsh attack on another computer user, written in a *newsgroup*, *message board* or *chat room*.

folder A computer *file* in which other files are stored, in order to keep them organized.

font The design of lettering for use in documents for screen or printed out.

forum Another name for a *message board*.

freeware *Software* that can be used for free.

FTP (File Transfer Protocol) A format used for the transfer of *data* between computers.

G

gigabyte (G or GB) A measurement of *data*, equivalent to 1,024 *Megabytes*.

graphics In computer terms, pictures displayed on the screen.

H

hacker (or **cracker**) A person who gains unauthorized access to a computer system, to steal, destroy or corrupt *files*.

hard copy A paper print-out of a document.

hardware The physical components of a computer that enable it to process *data*, plus its case, the mouse, keyboard, screen, and connecting cables.

History A list of recently visited *Web sites*, stored in a *folder* by Microsoft® Internet Explorer, to enable quick access to them at a later date.

home page 1) The *Web page* that displays first when you open your *browser*. 2) The main page of a *Web site*, which displays information about the contents of the site, and from which you can access all other pages.

HTML (HyperText Mark-up Language) The computer code used to create *Web pages*.

HTTP (HyperText Transfer Protocol) The code computers use to send pages across the *Internet*.

hyperlink A piece of text or an image that acts as a link from one *Web page* to another.

I

icon A small picture that represents a file.
index A type of *search engine* that lists millions of *Web sites*, and selects them by matching specified words.
Internet The vast computer *network* made by linking computers together around the world.
Internet service provider (ISP) A company that gives users access to the *Internet*.
Intranet A private Internet-style network, used, for example, by private companies.
IP address (Internet Protocol address) A number sequence recognized by computers which corresponds to a Web site's *domain name*. For example, the IP address of www.usborne.com is 212.67.205.134
ISDN (Integrated Services Digital Network) A type of *Internet* connection which can transfer *data* about three times as quickly as the speed of a standard *modem*.

J

Java A type of computer programming code. It is popular as a code for creating programs to run on the *Internet*. It is used to create *applets*.

K

Kilobyte (**K or Kb**) 1) A measurement of *data*, equivalent to 1,024 *bytes,* but often used loosely, to mean 1,000 bytes. 2) A measurement of *data transfer*, equivalent to 1,000 *bytes*, which is sometimes represented by a lower-case "k", for example 1000k.
K or **Kbps** (**Kilobits per second**) A thousand *bits* per second (*bps*). A measure of *connection speed*. For example, a "56K" modem has a maximum connection speed of 56,000 bps.

L

LAN (**Local Area Network**) A small *network*, usually within a single room or building.
link Abbreviation of *hyperlink*.
lurk To read the messages in a *chat room* or *newsgroup*, without *posting* any yourself.

M

margins The blank spaces around the edges of a document.
MB *Megabyte*.
Megabyte (**MB**) 1) A measurement of *data*, equivalent to 1,048,576 *bytes*.
2) A measurement of *data transfer*, equivalent to one million *bytes*.
message board A section of a *Web site* where users can leave and read comments and queries.
metasearcher A *search engine* that collects results from other search engines.
modem The basic device that enables a computer to send and receive *data* using phone lines.

N

netiquette The rules of polite conduct on the *Internet*.
network A group of computers, linked so that they can share information and resources.
newbie A new *Internet* user or a new member of a *newsgroup*.
newsgroup A discussion group operated over the *Internet*, often dedicated to a certain topic. Users *post* messages and can view others' responses.

O

offline Disconnected from the *Internet*.
online Connected to the *Internet*.
online service An *Internet Service Provider* that offers additional services to its subscribers, such as news and *instant messaging* facilities.
operating system The *software* that controls how a computer works, for example, the Microsoft® Windows® operating system.
operators Short for Boolean operators: words such as AND, OR and NOT, or symbols such as + and -, which are used to make *search engine* queries more specific.
orientation The direction in which a document is laid out on paper or screen – *portrait* (tall) or *landscape* (wide).

P

paste To copy text or an image from a computer's *clipboard* into a document.

PDF (**Portable Document Format**) A type of *file* which is a snapshot of a document. PDF files can be sent quickly over the *Web*, and viewed accurately using Adobe® Acrobat® Reader.

plug-in A *program* that works with your *browser* to give it extra features, such as enabling you to play video clips.

pop-up A small window, usually containing an advertisement, that appears on your screen when you *download* certain *Web pages*.

post To send a message to a *newsgroup*.

program A set of coded instructions telling a computer to perform a certain task.

protocol name The first part of a *URL*, which shows the code in which an *Internet* document is sent, for example, *HTTP*.

R

reboot To restart a computer.

routers Powerful computers owned by *ISPs* which sort and send *data* between *servers* and user computers.

S

search engine A *program* that searches for pages on the *Internet* containing certain specified words.

server A computer at the heart of a *network*, which stores *data* accessed by other (*client*) computers. A Web server stores *Web sites*.

shareware Software that can be tried out free of charge for a fixed period, on the understanding that a small fee is paid at the end of that time, if the software is retained.

software Computer *programs*, which enable you to perform tasks on a computer. **spam** Junk *e-mail*.

Streaming A technique for sending large documents over the Internet, where the file can be opened and used before it finishes its *download*.

T

trialware *Software* that can be *downloaded* and tried out without charge, but disables itself after a fixed period.

U

URL (**Uniform Resource Locator**) The unique address of any *Internet* document. For example, http://www.usborne.com/index.html

username A name that you choose to identify yourself when you are using the *Internet*.

V

Virtual Reality (**VR**) The use of 3-D *graphics* to create real looking objects and scenes which can be viewed from different angles.

virus A *program* which damages a computer by changing or deleting stored *data*.

W

WAN (**Wide Area Network**) A group of *LANs*, connected over a large geographical area.

Web page A document on the *World Wide Web*, which may contain graphics.

Web site A collection of *Web pages* put onto the Internet by an individual or organization, usually stored on the same *server*.

Webcam A camera that takes pictures, often live, which can be viewed on a Web site.

WinZip® Popular file-*compression* software. *Files* are compressed together into single files called Zip archives for easy transportation.

word processor An *application* which allows a user to work on text documents before printing them out. Many word processors also allow images to be inserted into documents.

World Wide Web (**WWW** or **Web**) A huge *network* on the *Internet* where documents containing graphics can be displayed.

X

xDSL The term used to describe all types of *DSL*, such as *ADSL*.

Useful extras

Here are some extras to top off your Internet skills. Read this page for tips on maintaining your Microsoft® Internet Explorer browser, streamlining its performance, speeding up your browsing, and brightening up your messages.

Setting your start page

To set a new start page in Microsoft Internet Explorer, go to the menu bar, click on **Tools**, then **Internet Options**, and choose the tab marked **General**. In the box, type in the address of the Web page you want and click on **Apply**.

Handling your History folder

To avoid being swamped by a History folder full of Web addresses, set the number of days of sites you'd like it to show. To start, use your right-hand mouse button to click on the **Internet Explorer** icon on your desktop.

Choose **Properties**. A window, called **Internet Properties**, will display. Near the bottom of this is a section called History. Look for a phrase saying "Days to keep pages in history:". Set the number of days that you wish to be remembered by typing the number you want in the little box next to the phrase.

Open a new window

Sometimes, you may find that you want to click on a hyperlink, but you'd prefer the link to open in a new window. This may be so that you can refer to the two documents at once, or so that you can continue reading the first Web page while the second opens, or whatever. To make a hyperlink open in a new window.

① Click on the hyperlink with your right-hand mouse button. A menu will appear.

② Click on the option that says **Open Link in New Window**. Hey presto! The link opens in a new window.

Speed up

You can speed up your use of Microsoft Internet Explorer by using what are known as keyboard shortcuts. Click on the commands **File** and **Edit** at the top of Microsoft Internet Explorer, and you'll see that some of the commands that appear in the drop-down menus have **Ctrl+** and a letter after them. This means that you can carry out the command by using just the keyboard, rather than clicking with your mouse.

To use these shortcuts, hold down the key marked **Ctrl** (it stands for "control") at the bottom-left of your keyboard and press the appropriate letter for each shortcut. The task will perform without you having to do any more clicking with your mouse.

This technique may seem strange, and at first it may take longer to perform functions. Persevere, though, and you'll find that it really does save lots of time, once you can remember which letter triggers which function.

Emoticons

Emoticons look like little faces, on their sides. They are made of punctuation marks. You may see them in e-mails or chat room messages.

Emoticons help to convey the emotion behind the words in a message. They can be especially useful when you are trying to swap homework information with somebody you've never met before. They help to explain the tone of the message that you have just written. Here are some that you could use.

:-)	*Happy*	:^D	*Great!*
:-D	*Laughing*	:-@	*Screaming*
:'-)	*Crying with laughter*	:-O	*Wow!*
:-(	*Sad*	:-&	*Tongue tied*
:'-(	*Very sad*	l-O	*Yawning*
;-)	*Winking*	\o/	*Hallelujah!*
:*)	*Clowning around*	:-P	*Tongue out*

Index

Acknowledgements

With thanks to Lisa Watts, Usborne Web site manager.

Every effort has been made to trace the copyright holders of the material in this book. If any rights have been omitted, the publishers offer their sincere apologies and will rectify this in any future edition, following notification. The publishers are grateful to the following organizations and individuals for their contribution and permission to reproduce material.

Windows® applications screenshots used courtesy of Microsoft Corporation. Windows®, Microsoft® Windows® 98, Microsoft® Windows® Me, Microsoft® Encarta® Encyclopedia, Microsoft® Internet Explorer and Microsoft® Outlook Express are either registered trademarks or trademarks of Microsoft Corporation in the US and/or other countries.

Cover Ask Jeeves is a registered trademark of Ask Jeeves, Inc. The Jeeves design and Ask.com are service marks of Ask Jeeves, Inc. Used with permission. (Also used on p18.) *www.ask.com*
Surfmonkey logo used with permission. (Also used on p23.) *www.surfmonkey.com*
p2-3 Background ©EyeWire.
p4-5 BrainPop screenshot used with permission. *www.brainpop.com*
Curiosos screenshot used with permission. *www.curiosos.com*
Map of Washington DC used by permission of Ray Sterner, The John Hopkins University Applied Physics Laboratory. *jhuapl.edu*
National Gallery of Canada screenshot used with permission. *national.gallery.ca*
Amazon.com is a registered trademark of Amazon.com, Inc. Brand logo used with permission. *www.amazon.com*
WinZip is a registered trademark of WinZip Computing, Inc. Brand logo used with permission. (Also used on p51.) *www.winzip.com*
The Real logo is a registered trademark of RealNetworks, Inc. Used with permission. *www.real.com*
Assorted images ©Digital Vision. *www.digitalvisiononline.co.uk*
p8-9 De Digitale School screenshot. Used with permission. *www.digischool.nl*
KidsHealth.org screenshot used with permission. *www.kidshealth.org*
©2000 Moskitown screenshot and logo (also p32) are owned by Vivendi Universal Interactive Publishing International and are used in its educational Internet site *www.education.com* All rights reserved.
The Microsoft® Internet Explorer logo is a registered trademark of Microsoft Corporation in the US and/or other countries. (Also used on p10.) *www.microsoft.com*
Musée National de Moyen Age screenshots used with permission. *www.musee-moyenage.fr*
p14-15 Microsoft Download Center banner ©Microsoft Corporation. *www.microsoft.com*
The Adobe logo is a registered trademark of Adobe Systems Incorporated in the United States and/or other countries. *www.adobe.com*
Macromedia is a registered trademark of Macromedia, Inc. in the United States and/or other countries. *www.macromedia.com*
Espace Téléchargement banner ©Microsoft Corporation. *www.microsoft.com*

iPIX banner used with permission. *www.ipix.com*
Kids Domain banner used with permission. *www.kidsdomain.com*
Tucows banner used with permission. *www.tucows.com*
p16-17 The Yahoo!® logo is a registered trademark of Yahoo! Inc. *www.yahoo.com*
Google® brand features are trademarks of Google, Inc. Google logo used with permission. *www.google.com*
AltaVista® logo used with permission. *www.uk.altavista.com*
p18-19 WebFerret® logo used with permission. *www.ferretsoft.com*
Bingooo® screenshot used with permission. *www.bingooo.com*
Copernic® logo used with permission. *www.copernic.com*
p20-21 Assorted screenshots used courtesy of NASA. Also on p 22. *www.nasa.gov*
Mundo Astronomía screenshot used with permission. *www.mundoastronomia.com*
Various images ©Digital Vision. *www.digitalvisiononline.co.uk*
p22-23 Balloons screenshots used with permission. *www.kubicekballoons.cz*
German Space Net screenshot used courtesy of *www.raumfahrt.de*
AstroRED screenshot used with permission. *www.astrored.net/iss*
Ithaki for Kids logo used with permission. *ithaki.net/kids*.
The Yahoo!® Japan logo is a registered trademark of Yahoo! Japan Corporation. *www.yahoo.co.jp*
Ask Jeeves Kids and the Ask Jeeves Kids logo are service marks or trademarks of Ask Jeeves, Inc. Used with permission. *www.ajkids.com*
Indexplorian logo used with permission. *www.explorian.com*
Education World logo used with permission. *www.educationworld.com*.
Milkmoon logo used with permission. *www.milkmoon.de*
p24-25 Momes.net logo used with permission. *www.momes.net*
Contigo Santillana screenshot used courtesy of *www.santillana.es*
Learn.co.uk logo used with permission of Guardian Newspapers Ltd. *www.learn.co.uk*
Dicorama.com logo used courtesy of *www.dicorama.com*
Microsoft® Encarta® and the Encarta logo are trademarks or registered trademarks of Microsoft Corporation in the US and/or other countries. *www.microsoft.com*
L'Atlas national du Canada banner used with permission. *atlas.gc.ca*
Britannica.com logo used with permission of *www.britannica.com*
Fact Monster logo and design (also p28) are used by permission of *www.factmonster.com*
p28-29 Microsoft® Encarta® screenshot ©Microsoft Corporation. *www.microsoft.com*
WebEncyclo screenshot used courtesy of *www.webencyclo.fr*
YourDictionary.com screenshots used with permission. *www.yourdictionary.com*
InfoPlease screenshot used courtesy of *www.infoplease.com*
London street map screenshot used by permission of *www.streetmap.co.uk*

Map ©Bartholomews Map.
Australia map used courtesy of *www.maps.com*
Paris Metro map used courtesy of *www.ratp.fr*
America map screenshot used by permission of *www.mediamaps.com*
p30-31 BJ Pinchbeck Homework Helper screenshot used by permission of DiscoverySchool.com. *discoveryschool.com*
Cyberpapy screenshot used courtesy of *www.cyberpapy.com*
Homework High screenshot used by permission of *www.homeworkhigh.com*
p32-33 estudio24.com logo used by permission of *www.estudio24.com*
ILN logo used used courtesy of Future Graph, Inc. *www.iln.net*
p34-35 Howstuffworks screenshots used courtesy of *www.howstuffworks.com*
p36-37 Classroom Clipart screenshots used by permission of *www.classroomclipart.com*
Free Clipart Island images used by permission of *www.freeclipartisland.com*. Artist: Adrea Satre.
SchoolDiscovery.com images used with permission. *school.discovery.com*
Assorted images ©Digital Vision. *www.digitalvisiononline.co.uk*
p38-39 Volcano explanation screenshots used by permission of Dr. Vic Camp, Department of Geological Sciences, San Diego State University. *www.geology.sdsu.edu*
Volcanic eruption images ©Digital Vision.
p42-43 Background ©Stuart Westmoreland/CORBIS.
Shark Realities screenshot used by permission of Discovery Communications, Inc. *www.discovery.com*
Shark diagram ©EnchantedLearning.com. Used with permission. *www.enchantedlearning.com*
Shark jaws photo ©Graham Lambert. Used with permission.
Teeth comparisons picture used by permission of *www.sharkfriends.com*
Shark quotation used by permission of Mike Chew.
p44-45 Sunflower photo ©Digital Vision.
p48-49 Tiger, child & landscape photos ©Digital Vision.
p52-53 Image of Iomega® Zip® disks used by permission of Iomega International S.A. *www.iomega.com*
Images of Sony media used by permission of Sony UK Ltd. *www.sony.co.uk*
p56-57 Cyber Patrol® logo used by permission of SurfControl plc. *www.surfcontrol.com*
Net Nanny® logo used by permission of Net Nanny Software, Inc. *www.netnanny.com*
Norton AntiVirus® 2001 (Chinese) logo used courtesy of Symantec Corporation. *www.symantec.com*.
McAfee logo used courtesy of McAfee.com Corporation. *www.mcafee.com*.
p1,4-41,44-64 Background images ©Digital Vision. *www.digitalvisiononline.co.uk*

Usborne Publishing are not responsible and do not accept liability for the availability or content of any Web site other than our own, or for any exposure to harmful, offensive, or inaccurate material which may appear on the Web. Usborne Publishing have no liability for any damage or loss caused by viruses that may be downloaded as a result of browsing the sites we recommend. Usborne downloadable pictures are copyright of Usborne Publishing Ltd and may not be reproduced in print or in electronic form for any commercial or profit-related purpose.